The New World Order and the Third World

The New World Order and the Third World

• edited by Dave Broad and Lori Foster •

Montréal/New York

Copyright © 1992. All rights reserved by the individual authors. Essay by Samir Amin, Copyright © 1991 by the Monthly Review Foundation.

No part of this book may be reproduced or transmitted in any form, by any means, electronic or mechanical, including photocopying and recording, or by any information storage or retrieval system, without written permission from the publisher, except for brief passages quoted by a reviewer in a newspaper or magazine.

BLACK ROSE BOOKS No. V170
Hardcover ISBN: 1-895431-17-4
Paperback ISBN: 1-895431-16-6

Canadian Cataloguing in Publication Data

Main entry under title:

The New World Order and the Third World

ISBN 1-895431-17-4 (bound) — ISBN 1-895431-16-6 (pbk.)

1. International relations — Forecasting. 2. United States — Foreign relations — 1989 — Forecasting. 3. United States — Foreign relations — 1945 — 4. United States — Foreign relations — Developing countries — Forecasting. I. Broad, Dave II. Foster, Lori

D849.N49 1991   327.73'009'04901   C91-090491-X

Library of Congress Catalog No. 91-72978

Cover Design: Werner Arnold

Mailing Address

BLACK ROSE BOOKS
C.P. 1258
Succ. Place du Parc
Montréal, Québec
H2W 2R3 Canada

BLACK ROSE BOOKS
340 Nagel Drive
Cheektowaga, New York
14225 USA

A publication of the Institute of Policy Alternatives of Montréal (IPAM)

Printed in Canada

*To the billions of victims of the 'New World Order'
…North, South, East and West…*

Contents

Notes on Contributors ix
Editors' Preface xi
Introduction: Cold War, Hot War, What More?
   Dave Broad, Lori Foster and Joe Roberts 1

Part I: A "New World Order"?

1. U.S. Sponsorship of International Terrorism
   Edward S. Herman 17

2. Beyond Rollback: U.S. Foreign Policy into the 1990s
   Robert Gould and Thomas Bodenheimer 41

3. The Real Stakes in the Gulf War
   Samir Amin 69

Part II: Whither The Revolutions?

4. Central America in Transition: Between an Imperial Past and an Uncertain Future
   Susanne Jonas 81

5. U.S. Imperialism and Nicaragua: Did the Contras Lose the War but Win the Election?
   David Close 95

6. The Privatization of War: Low Intensity Imperialism in the Philippines
   Douglas W. Booker 117

7. Revolution, Counterrevolution and Imperialism: La Lucha Continua!
   Dave Broad 143

Notes on Contributors

Samir Amin is Director of the African Office of Third World Forum in Dakar, Senegal. He is author and co-author of numerous studies of imperialism and world politics, including *Delinking: Towards a Polycentric World* (Zed Books), and *Transforming the Revolution: Social Movements and the World-System* (Monthly Review Press).

Thomas Bodenheimer is a medical doctor in San Francisco, California who has been active in anti-imperialist activities for many years. He has written many articles on health policy and U.S. foreign affairs, and is co-author of *Rollback!: Right-wing Power in U.S. Foreign Policy* (South End Press).

Douglas W. Booker is an Ottawa-based researcher who has lived and worked in the Philippines. He has been active in Third World solidarity and trade union work, and is currently working on a study of Philippine women workers in transnational free trade zones.

Dave Broad teaches sociology and anthropology at Memorial University in Corner Brook, Newfoundland. He has had a long interest in imperialism and national liberation struggles, and has published a number of articles on these subjects. He is presently completing a study of global economic restructuring and its impact on labour markets in centre states.

David Close teaches political science at Memorial University in St. John's, Newfoundland. He has spent some years studying the Nicaraguan revolution, and is author of *Nicaragua: Politics, Economics and Society* (Frances Pinter).

Lori Foster is a freelance journalist living in Corner Brook, Newfoundland. She has been active in Third World solidarity and struggles for social justice. Currently she is helping to set up a food bank and cooperative for victims of the "new world order."

Robert Gould is a medical doctor in San Francisco, California who is active in Physicians for Social Responsibility. He has had a long interest in U.S. foreign policy, and is co-author of *Rollback!: Right-wing Power in U.S. Foreign Policy* (South End Press).

Edward S. Herman is Professor of Finance at the Wharton School of the University of Pennsylvania, and editor of *Lies of Our Times*. He is author and co-author of many works on U.S. imperialism and human rights, including *The Political Economy of Human Rights* (Black Rose Books); *The Real Terror Network: Terrorism in Fact and Propaganda* (Black Rose Books); and *The "Terrorism" Industry: The Experts and Institutions that Shape Our View of Terror* (Pantheon Books).

Susanne Jonas teaches Latin American Studies at the University of California at Santa Cruz, and is an editor of *Social Justice*. She has authored and co-authored numerous books on U.S. imperialism and Latin America, including *Democracy in Latin America: Visions and Realities* (Bergin & Garvey Publishers); and *The Battle for Guatemala: Rebels, Death Squads and U.S. Power* (Westview Press).

Joe Roberts teaches political science at the University of Regina, Saskatchewan, and has studied U.S. imperialism for many years. He is editor of *The Crisis in Socialist Theory, Strategy and Practice* (Garamond Press); and is presently completing a book on the history of social democracy.

Editors' Preface

This collection grew out of sessions on Third World revolution and counterrevolution which were organized for the Canadian Learned Societies Conferences in Québec City and Victoria, B.C., in the springs of 1989 and 1990, respectively. The sessions were organized by and for scholars who not only study political movements in the Third World, but do so as part of their own political work as solidarity activists. The contributions published here as Part II were presented at those sessions. The chapters in Part I were solicited to provide an overview of U.S. imperialism. It is our hope that this collection will help readers to penetrate the rhetoric of a "new world order," and provide a tool for political action against that supposed order.

We wish to thank all of the contributors whose work has made this volume possible. We especially thank Doug Booker and Lorne Brown for pushing the project along. And we would be terribly remiss if we did not thank the office staff at Grenfell College for preparing the manuscript.

Introduction

Cold War, Hot War, What More?*

Dave Broad, Lori Foster and Joe Roberts

> *It is my duty...to prevent, by the independence of Cuba, the United States from spreading over the West Indies and falling with that added weight upon other lands of our America....I have lived inside the monster [United States] and know its entrails.*
>
> Last letter written by José Marti, hero of Cuban independence.

Our world has just been rocked by two momentous "events" — "the end of the Cold War," and the so-called Gulf War against Iraq. These are signs of what the U.S. government calls a "new world order." We have seen the consequences of these events for populations in areas immediately affected. But no less dramatic effects are already being felt by others further away. Our particular concern in this volume is to assess the nature of the new world order and map the trajectory of Third World emancipation. The contributors analyze the problems and possibilities for Third World revolutions and social movements in confronting a not-so-new world

---

* Parts of this introduction are adapted from an article published in *Monthly Review*, Vol. 41, No. 7 (December 1989).

order. They take us inside continuing struggles against "the monster," as José Marti called it, and show the potential for a really new and humane world order.

Imperialism After the Cold War

Paul Sweezy,[1] for one, asserts that the year 1989 will go down in history. Most significant is the downfall of the old authoritarian regimes of Eastern Europe, capped by the knocking down of the Berlin Wall. Eastern Europe is now going into pluralistic politics and full market economics, with the centre of the Soviet Union rapidly following suit.

Western pundits now talk about the "triumph of capitalism"[2] and the "end of history."[3] This reminds us of Daniel Bell's very ideological pronouncement of an "end of ideology" at the end of the 1950s[4] — the height of the post-World War II economic boom. The radical upheavals of the 1960s quickly proved Bell wrong. And we suspect that those who have pronounced the end of socialism and/or communism will be proven wrong as well. Moreover, it would be brash for any of us to say exactly what is in store. Even if communism[5] is on the long-term agenda, that agenda is yet to be written.

It seems arguable that it is too early to assert the end of a social system — socialism or communism — which had never really been achieved.[6] There has been great debate on the Left as to the character of the old East European regimes — were they "state capitalist," "state collectivist," "state socialist...?" But the common adjective "state" tells us that many on the Left have not been satisfied that these regimes easily qualified as socialist or communist. Many have simply written them off as "Stalinist dictatorships."

Whichever of these positions one might take, it leads to a different position than that of the liberal and conservative ideologues cited above. Even if it looks to some of us that, in practice, Eastern rulers are engaged in returning their countries to the capitalist fold, the "collectivist" heritage of the peoples there suggests that this may not be the final outcome. Popular demonstrations and strikes against the higher costs of living and rising unemployment that reunification of the two Germanies has brought to the East serve as examples.

Often ignored in these discussions is the current situation of the so-called Third World. Socialism has been held out as the great hope for the peoples on the periphery of the world capitalist system, who have long suffered under exploitation and oppression. But even the press is now asking about the fate of these peoples, as the "Soviet model" collapses and former Eastern benefactors of the Third World increasingly look simultaneously westward and inward.

During the entire period since the Second World War peoples of the periphery have been engaged in a titanic struggle for national autonomy and development. Although the rhetoric of imperialism has always proclaimed that the enemy of the periphery is communism which ultimately emanates from Moscow, this has from the start been recognized as a smoke-screen by the Third World peoples and even many of its leaders. To the degree that the former U.S.S.R. discontinues its ideological and military support for struggles of liberation, the new directions seem to be constraining the liberation process (see Jonas and Broad below).

Certainly the United States has had to modify its anti-Soviet rationale for counter-revolutionary activity in the periphery (see Chapter Seven), but there is no reason to believe it will cease or diminish its crusade to control the markets and politics of the periphery, as the invasion of Panama and the Gulf War clearly show. Indeed, whether we examine the worsening terms of commodity and capital trade, the price to the periphery of debt, the institutional and policy changes imposed by the World Bank and the International Monetary Fund (IMF), the retreat of private lenders, or the continuing instigation of regional conflicts and surrogate warfare inspired by the United States, along with the threat of more direct interventions, there has been no ray of hope for the periphery in the easing of superpower tensions.

In fact there is reason to fear that the increase of bloc rivalries between the European Community, the United States/Canada, and Japan — the classical imperialist rivalries leading to redivision of world markets and ultimately to war — poses more long-term danger, the appearance of a new alliance under U.S. hegemony notwithstanding.

While the United States dominated the capitalist world, it could exercise some discipline over competition and rivalry through international development, trade, and political agencies. As that hegemony has eroded since the early 1970s, there are no monetary and trade bodies capable of enforcing order; the mediating functions of IMF and the General Agreement on Tariffs and Trade (GATT) are similarly deteriorating. The relations between the centre and the periphery can become even more chaotic than at present with each nation or bloc seeking to maximize its domination and exploitation of preferred sectors of the periphery.

Thus, while the United States may be forced to withdraw its involvement in certain parts of the periphery from time to time, its continuing dependence on resources and consumer markets, cheap labor, and investment openings will require a continued presence in its historic hinterlands. And methods for enforcing compliance and order in those regions have become more sophisticated since the U.S. defeat in Vietnam.

Where it is politically feasible, as in Panama and Iraq, the United States will sustain its cowboy adventures of invasion and capture. But the preferred means of dominating unchanging conditions continues to include efforts to co-opt local comprador classes through government and military interaction, along with active efforts in this direction by transnational corporations and banks; exploiting the educational system to subvert youth militancy; the counterattack against religious radicalism in the periphery; intensification of media ideological saturation, including greater use of culture and sport to defuse opposition; and more focused application of CIA and other intelligence methods to anticipate, confuse, intimidate, divide, and discourage resistance is probable, with increased funding for so-called low-intensity warfare.

If we include the objective constraint on policy alternatives which the dependency relation imposes on peripheral rulers, any serious depression for the economies of the centre can be expected to have disastrous consequences for the periphery. Indeed the stagnant growth of the 1980s has already sent the periphery into depression. The return to dictatorships generally in America's preferred hinterland might not be as desirable as installation of such plausible friends as Madame Chamorro, Madame Bhutto and Madame Aquino, but dictator allies are much preferable to socialist or nationalist independence governments (see Chapter One).

What remains constant are the requirements that transcend economic and political transformations in the East. According to John Bellamy Foster, "the long term, organic crisis of accumulation as it is manifested in our time can be characterized as stagnation and financial explosion in the centre, along with the increasingly destabilizing effects of imperialist underdevelopment in the periphery."[7] The U.S. government has pronounced a new world order in the wake of the Gulf War. The governing principle of this supposed new order in the West is political-economic "restructuring" according to neo-liberal market principles. These same principles now appear to dominate what remains of "Perestroika" in the East. In the South, as Amin[8] has noted, peoples of the Third World are subject to IMF and World Bank inspired "structural adjustments" to the North's "restructuring." A "peripheralization" of the East appears to be producing similar "structural adjustments."[9] Given these conditions, Foster's conclusion to a review of Joyce Kolko's *Restructuring the World Economy*[10] is appropriate: "Thus restructuring will lead to rising revolts by the external [peripheral] proletariat, at a time when the advanced capitalist system is also in the process of undermining the myth of the middle class and thus of the integration of its internal proletariat."[11]

The Gulf War: High Intensity Conflict

There was a general feeling of hope among most people in the Western world that the confrontation between the United States and the Soviet Union which has dominated world development since the Second World War would abate, and that a new era less prone to the anxiety of war would emerge. But this hope was to be short lived. First, in December of 1989, the United States invaded Panama. Then in August of 1990, Iraq invaded Kuwait, for various cultural, economic and political reasons of which most Westerners remain ignorant.[12] The United States and its allies found this invasion the perfect pretext for their own invasion of Iraq in January of 1991, under the guise of United Nations' sponsorship.

The supposed United Nations' forces were little more than a front for the U.S. The Western mainstream media fell into line behind their States in portraying the Gulf War as a replay of World War II. But there are some fundamental differences. Saddam Hussein may not be an admirable fellow, but despite the self-serving accusations of George Bush, neither is Hussein "Adolf Hitler revisited." And the Gulf War was not an inter-imperialist war, at least on the military front, but rather an imperialist assault on a Third World State whose pretensions were to become a regional power.

The inter-imperialist element to the war was economic. The U.S. economy is in decline, relative to especially Germany and Japan, and

U.S. hopes for retaining and perhaps expanding its "spheres of influence" in the Third World are based on military might (see Chapter Two). But U.S. interests have also been partially reined in by Third World resistance.

The right-wing political and military rulers surrounding George Bush thought they were going to have a quick and easy time of defeating Saddam Hussein's army, but it was necessary to "bomb Iraq back to the Stone Age" to avoid a "costly" ground war. The cost, of course, was borne by the Iraqis. The extent of material damage and civilian casualties (euphemistically called "collateral damage") caused by the bombs of the "civilized" West was so great, any estimate is incomplete. Even as Iraqi military and civilian personnel were finally retreating from Kuwait they were bombarded so heavily that the road from Kuwait City to the Iraqi border was littered with over 100,000 corpses and miles of burned-out vehicles. One Western pilot commented that it was like a "duck shoot." Was this necessary? The criminal bombing raids that the "allies" rained on Iraq certainly reinforced anti-Yankee sentiments in that country, and spread them around the Arab world. Even those states of the Maghreb in northern Africa which supported the U.S./U.N. coalition have had to confront a restless populace who sympathize with Iraq.

Many of the common folk in the Arab world sided with Saddam Hussein in his invasion of Kuwait, because they had no love for the elite rulers of the old emirate. And they would probably have supported the overthrow of the Saudi emirate as well, though we remain sceptical about the White House's scare-mongering that Hussein had any original intention of such an act. The man may be unsavoury and ambitious, but he is obviously not stupid. In fact, as the war continued Hussein came to look like something of a hero to many Arabs for his "anti-imperialism." And his stature grew in other parts of the Third World where there were many pro-Iraqi demonstrations.

On Wednesday, February 27, 1991 U.S. President Bush, not U.N. Secretary General Perez de Cuellar, announced that the Gulf War was over. This was after a flurry of efforts by Soviet diplomats to negotiate a peace with the Iraqi regime through the U.N. Security Council. But the United States had little time for this. The U.N. was only a useful expedient for the United States to get its war started. And U.S. rulers could hardly allow the Soviets to gain either prestige or more influence in the Persian

Gulf. Iraq had to be defeated on U.S. terms. It would appear that the Cold War was not yet over.

So, during one last orgy of bombing, George Bush announced his victory. Noam Chomsky, being interviewed for CBC Television's The Journal (01/03/91), noted that the war was necessary for the U.S. to achieve their interests. First of all, U.S. corporate oil profits had to be protected. Moreover, since the Second World War, the United States has maintained its hegemonic power by force. Force had to be used to teach an upstart Third World regime that it had gone too far.

The lesson for other Third World States is that they will suffer a similar fate if they step too far out of line. And the history of such lessons reveals that the character of Saddam Hussein was not the central issue. Other imperial powers, especially Britain and France, went along with the United States because they have their own interests to protect, and cannot let the United States run the whole show.

Having incurred relatively few casualties on his side, Bush boasted that the United States could "kick the Vietnam Syndrome once and for all." But the U.S. government has opened up a can of worms for itself. The repercussions from their invasion of Iraq will be felt in Gulf politics for a long time. The hypocrisy of calling for U.N.-sponsored actions to confront Iraqi aggression when no such actions have been taken against Israel for its ongoing aggressions and annexations of Arab territories is plain for all to see.[13] Bush's release of more military aid to El Salvador while the world was focused on the Middle East, and decrying of Iraqi human rights abuses while blithely ignoring criticisms of human rights abuses by U.S. allies in Latin America and elsewhere are cynical acts of imperialism.[14]

Having gone from Cold War to hot war in the Persian Gulf, we must now ask: "What more?" It would appear that if things are left to George Bush and his team we are in for more of the same. With the Gulf War now fading from view in the West it seems that the U.S. government must concoct other pretexts for exercising their military might to maintain global hegemony. The latest ruse comes in the form of charges laid against two Libyan intelligence agents for the bombing of Pan American Flight 103, which crashed in Lockerbie, Scotland on December 21, 1988. The argument of U.S. and British officials is that the Pan Am flight was bombed by Libya in retaliation for President Reagan's 1986 air attacks on Libya.

Libyan leader Moammar Gadhafi is said to have ordered the bombing. So the U.S. has a convenient "terrorist" target for sabre-rattling.[15] U.S. and British authorities are demanding that Libya hand over the two suspects. If not, says White House spokesman Marlin Fitzwater, "We are considering action and I'll leave it at that. We don't rule out any option."[16]

Even if the Libyan agents were involved in the bombing, this seems all too convenient an excuse for President Bush to continue riding his war horse. And we should indeed question the choice of target. "A lot of people thought it was Syrians," said Bush in a speech. "The Syrians took a bum rap on this."[17] We are led to wonder why it is Libya, which opposed the U.S. war on Iraq, that has become the target in the Lockerbie case, and not Syria, a former foe of the United States which turned to support the United States in the Gulf War. But we should not wonder too long. The more important question is why U.S. militarism must continue. And the answer lies in the continuing decline of U.S. hegemony, continuing stagnation in the U.S. economy, the power of the U.S. military-industrial elite to influence U.S. foreign policy (see Chapter Two), and continuation of Third World anti-imperialist struggles (see Chapters Four through Seven below).

Black as things seem for the Third World, we must remember that resurgence of U.S. imperialism is due largely to the loss of U.S. global competitiveness, and inability and unwillingness to deal with social problems at home. The United States, supposedly the richest country on the planet, is decaying from within. In light of this, since U.S. rulers have no obvious interest in social reforms at home, foreign military adventures, as part of a quest to salvage a declining empire, make sense. George Bush's ratings in U.S. popular opinion polls ran over 90 percent immediately after the Gulf War. But, the military solution to the United States' economic and political woes will not work, as is suggested by recent protests against Bush's (lack of a) domestic economic programme.[18]

Imperialism versus Revolution

This volume brings together essays which will give readers important background for understanding George Bush's supposed new world order. Collectively, the essays ask what is really new in the new world order. Part I focuses on the role of the United States as the hegemonic power of the twentieth century, and on the impact of U.S. world orders, "old" and "new," on the Third World. Part II provides case studies of the impact of U.S. imperialism on the Third World, and focuses on the prospects for popular struggles.

In Chapter One, Edward Herman gives us an overview of assaults against national liberation struggles since the revolution of 1917 in Russia. He discusses how the U.S. has fashioned the foremost state terror network of this century. Herman explains how the United States has managed to define "terrorism" to its own benefit and spread "policies formerly applicable to the 'banana republics' of Central America...to the entire world."

The U.S. has aided and built up the forces of terrorism in four ways: by protecting and rehabilitating fascists; by outright or proxy invasions; by subversion aimed at overthrowing governments; and by "supplying repression" via financial aid, training and arms supply to security forces or military dictators. The 18 military takeovers in Latin America between 1960 and 1968 were a predictable result of the build up and "education" of Latin American armed forces. As well, Herman shows that as human rights conditions have deteriorated aid has increased, and the factors affecting the "climate of investment" for transnational corporations have improved. Herman concludes: "A good case can be made that socialism never had a chance in instances where it showed promise, as a result of Western-organized hostility and violence." None of this changes with Bush's new world order. So Herman tells us that U.S.-sponsored terrorism "can only be fought by a determined effort to understand the reality, to call it by its right names, and to organize to contest the hegemony of the dominant terrorists."

In Chapter Two, Robert Gould and Thomas Bodenheimer discuss post-World War II shifts in U.S. foreign policy. They note that two tendencies have competed in setting U.S. foreign policy; the Right-wing and the traditional conservative elites. While the traditional conservatives aimed to contain or prevent the spread of Soviet influence in the world, the Right pushed for global rollback and complete victory over communism — the sooner the better. While the United States was the top economic power in the world a policy of containment satisfied everyone, but as the United States started to lose ground some business interests pushed harder for rollback. By the late 1980s the Right was asserting more control.

The so-called Iran-Contra scandal, or Contragate, reflected the conflict between the two tendencies. However, as Bodenheimer and Gould point out, during Contragate neither side said the United States should mind its own business and get out of Nicaragua; they simply disagreed on the methods that should be used to rollback revolution.

Following Contragate aggressive rollback was held in check. The Bush administration returned foreign policy to the traditional leadership that strove to integrate the world and reserved the military option "for those who did not have the sense to know their place in the unfolding new world order." And while "sense" is being knocked into some, the Right is continuing to rollback socialism in the newly "liberated" countries of Eastern Europe. At the same time the traditional conservatives are concerned with American competitiveness, fearing that the United States is falling behind Europe and Japan. Gould and Bodenheimer conclude that "transnational elites, faced with the looming possibility of world economic collapse, will likely intensify the policies of austerity capitalism imposed by sheer force in the Third World, and progressively incorporate such policies to maintain rule at home."

In Chapter Three, Samir Amin outlines the real stakes in the Gulf War, and discusses the prospects for progressive social transformation throughout the world. Amin says the Gulf War heightened "the injustices that are the foundation of all world orders, new and old." The war in the Gulf was a North-South conflict — the Iraqi regime and the personality of Suddam Hussein were of secondary importance.

The last half of the 1980s saw an intensification of international capital's offensive to subordinate the Third World to the expansion of capitalism. As Amin notes: "The unification of the world by the market will not lead to peace, but, on the contrary, to the intensification of storms of violence against the victims of the market." The Gulf War was just the most recent act of violence in this struggle. Furthermore, Amin argues that the Gulf War will not result in U.S. hegemony but more likely in a triumvirate of the United States, Japan and Germany — the latter two knowing how to pay the United States to police the world. The war has not changed the world order, but prolonged the capitalist world order. What is required, according to Amin, is not hegemony but polycentrism, which will allow the development of progressive social struggles throughout the world.

In Chapter Four, Susanne Jonas looks at the effects that global political changes have had on Central America. She starts on an optimistic note, saying that even though there have been setbacks and many lives lost, advances have been made and the revolutionary processes have permanently transformed the region and its peoples.

However, after seeing the destruction in Nicaragua, the popular/revolutionary forces in El Salvador are talking about sharing rather than taking power. The near victories of left political parties in Brazilian and Mexican elections portend the spread of democratic models, but two negative developments militate against this. Economically, the debt crisis has caused extreme poverty and suffering, and the United States has again begun to use overt intervention.

The former U.S.S.R.'s commitment to domestic concerns implies a pulling back even further from support of Third World struggles. In the second half of the 1980s Western Europe had pushed for democracy and human rights in Latin America, but few material resources were offered. So the popular forces in Latin America can stay but not defeat the hand of imperialism.

Jonas closes by saying that the solidarity movement had some successes, but was unable to stop the contras or the invasion of Panama. If solidarity activists are to be successful we must demand the "peace dividend" for communities with poverty, joblessness and homelessness, rather than buying into the U.S. government's arguments about national security threats.

In Chapter Five, David Close discusses the 1990 electoral defeat of the Sandinistas in Nicaragua. Pointing out that Nicaragua is in Central America, the United States' "backyard," he looks at the ways the U.S. contributed to the defeat. The Sandinistas allowed freedom of association and expression, giving the opposition room to operate legally in the country. Close says this atmosphere allowed "low-intensity conflict" (LIC), used by the United States against Nicaragua, to be most effective.

However, the U.S. government did not necessarily beat the Sandinistas. Close makes the very important point that, if we lay all the blame for the defeat of the Sandinistas on the United States without criticizing the FSLN, "it makes imperialism appear invincible." He says: "There were things the FSLN could have done to salvage the vote, but they were unbelievably overconfident and badly misread the electorate....The 1990 elections showed the Sandinistas the importance of keeping in touch with their supporters": an important lesson for all popular struggles.

Low Intensity Conflict (LIC) has been used in undermining popular governments and movements all over the world. In Chapter Six, Douglas Booker shows that the fundamentalist churches have been very effective in whipping up anti-communist hysteria in the Philippines, as part of the LIC strategy against the Left. The LIC strategists have also facilitated the formation of vigilante groups which grew when the U.S. Congress halted aid to the contras in Central America and covert and private aid increased.

"This campaign of total war has been premised on bringing the convictions and resources of the private sector and private individuals into the conflict. The anti-communist network has played a fundamental role in establishing the conditions for launching grassroots warfare….The cases of Nicaragua and the Philippines demonstrate that these networks are important to the operationalization of a new foreign policy based on Low Intensity Conflict. In setting up networks of the New Right to carry out these objectives, it is possible to circumvent the roadblocks (e.g., Congress) to the reactionary rollback agenda."

However, Booker finds that there have been successes in spite of LIC and that the movement for democracy is gaining strength. In areas where the underground was greatly weakened after the overthrow of Marcos it has returned and is making headway. This is reflected in the recent vote in the Philippine Congress to revoke the U.S. lease on the Subic Bay naval base.

In Chapter Seven, Dave Broad sets the current conjuncture in historical context, giving a longer view of struggles between revolutionaries and counterrevolutionaries, and discussing the relevance of LIC and so-called "drug wars" to revolutionary transformations in the Third World. He points out that recent "democratic openings" are partial concessions to real demands for democracy and, in reference to Nicaragua, says that the hearts and minds of the people were not won in the 1990 election, their resistance was ground down. Broad notes that there are growing popular movements for social justice throughout the world, and says it is clear to many that capitalism has *not* delivered the goods. However, the decline of capitalism will be a lengthy process and, as we approach the 500th anniversary of Columbus' "discovery" of the "New World," more than ever "the choice appears to be between 'socialism and barbarism'."

Apropos this point is Russian socialist Boris Kagarlitsky's conclusion to a discussion of the Soviet revolution that

> the left all over the world now has to pay the price of its uncritical support and adulation of the Russian revolutionary tradition.
>
> On the other hand, there is an objective necessity to have a left different from what social democracy can offer. Social democracy is also exhausted, capitalism itself is exhausted. In a way the Russian and Eastern European experience once again shows that capitalism has nothing new or efficacious to propose. It demonstrates the extent to which capitalism has become exhausted worldwide. The need for an alternative is clearly there.[19]

Notes

1. Paul Sweezy, "Nineteen Eighty-Nine," Monthly Review, Vol.41, No.11, April 1990: pp. 18-21.
2. Robert Heilbroner, "The Triumph of Capitalism," *The New Yorker*, Vol.64, January 23, 1989: pp. 98-109.
3. Francis Fukuyama, "The End of History?," *The National Interest*, Vol. 16, Summer 1989: pp. 3-17.
4. Daniel Bell, *The End of Ideology*. Glencoe, Ill.: Free Press, 1960.
5. Here we are thinking of the distinction, often made by Marxists, between "socialism" as a transition phase and "communism" as the new social formation. Marx himself referred to first and second stages of communism.
6. Eduardo Galeano, "A Child Lost in the Storm," *The Guardian*, Vol.42, No.27, May 2, 1990: pp. 1, 12.
7. John Bellamy Foster, "Restructuring the World Economy in a Time of Lasting Crisis," *Monthly Review*, Vol.41, No.1, May 1989: p. 47.
8. Samir Amin, "The Future of Socialism," *Monthly Review*, Vol.42, No.3 (July-August 1990): pp. 10-29.
9. Saul Landau, "A New World to Exploit: The East Joins the South," *Monthly Review*, Vol.42, No.5, October 1990: pp. 29-37.
10. Joyce Kolko, *Restructuring the World Economy*. New York: Pantheon Books, 1988.
11. John Bellamy Foster, "Restructuring the World Economy in a Time of Lasting Crisis," *Monthly Review*, Vol.41, No. 1, May 1989: p. 54.
12. For background and discussion see Feroz Ahmad, "Arab Nationalism, Radicalism, and the Specter of Neocolonialism," *Monthly Review*, Vol.42, No.9, February 1991: pp. 30-37; Tom Mayer, "Imperialism and the Gulf War," *Monthly Review*, Vol.42, No.11, April, 1991: pp. 1-11.
13. See, for example, Norman G. Finkelstein, "Isreal and Iraq: A Double Standard in the Application of International Law," *Monthly Review*, Vol.43, No.3, July-August 1991: pp. 25-54.

14. See Chapter One below; and Edward S. Herman, "The United States versus Human Rights in the Third World," *Harvard Human Rights Journal*, Vol.4, Spring 1991: pp. 85-104.
15. On the mechanics of the targeting of "terrorists," see Chapter One below.
16. James Rowley, "Libyans Charged in Bombing Over Lockerbie," *The Globe and Mail*, Friday, November 15, 1991.
17. Ibid.
18. Arthur MacEwan, "Why the Emperor Can't Afford New Clothes: International Change and Fiscal Disorder in the United States," *Monthly Review*, Vol.43, No.3, July-August, 1991: pp. 74-94.
19. Interview with Fred Weir, "Yeltsin's Power Grab the Real Coup," *The Guardian*, Vol. 44, No. 2, October 30, 1991: p. 15.

Part I

A "New World Order"?

Chapter One

U.S. Sponsorship of International Terrorism*

Edward S. Herman

For the average citizen of the West, the idea of the United States as a sponsor of international terrorism — let alone the *dominant* sponsor, as I will argue below — would appear utterly incomprehensible. After all, one reads daily that the United States is leading the charge against something it calls "terrorism," and it even regularly assails its allies for dragging their feet in responding to terrorism. On the other hand, the U.S. government organized a mercenary army to attack Nicaragua, and even provided it with a printed manual of recommended acts of sabotage and murder, which was implemented by the proxy army, at the cost of thousands of civilian lives.[1] The U.S. Government has also long been "constructively engaged" with the apartheid government of South Africa, which in the years 1975-88 invaded, and organized its own mercenary armies, to subvert a string of frontline states, here at the cost of hundreds of thousands of civilian lives.[2] The Western media, however, never refer to the United States or South Africa as "terrorist states," even though both of them have killed vastly greater numbers than Gadhafi or the Red Brigades.[3]

The reason for the Western misperception is that *the powerful define terrorism,* and the Western media loyally follow the agenda of their own leaders. The powerful naturally define terrorism to exclude their own acts

---
* This chapter is a revised and updated version of an article published in *Social Justice,* No. 27-28, 1987.

and those of their friends and clients. They always portray themselves as the victims of terrorism, engaging in "retaliation" and "counterterror," whatever the facts.[4] This allows a remarkable role reversal in which, for example, throughout the 1980s the United States, South Africa and Guatemala were victims of terrorism, the Salvadoran and Guatemalan rebels and South Africa's African National Congress were terrorists.[5]

If one straightens out these roles and assesses the true locus of intimidation by violence and threat of violence on the global scene, it becomes clear that the United States, as the dominant and perhaps only *real* superpower, has been the supreme terrorist in recent decades.

U.S. Hegemony and the Role of Terror

A hegemonic power with enormous technological and financial resources has wide options in the use of both peaceable and violent means to accomplish its ends. The violent means include all of the various forms of terrorism, and the United States as hegemonic power has used — or sponsored the use of — all of them. In most of these modalities the United States is not unique, it is merely quantitatively important, sometimes outstandingly so.

(1) *Nuclear Terrorism.* The United States approaches uniqueness, however, in the use of the nuclear threat as a form of intimidation. The United States is the only country that has actually used nuclear weapons on enemy populations; not just one bomb, but two, destroying two substantial Japanese cities and exterminating several hundred thousand people in the process. It seems clear that this murderous destruction was unnecessary, that Japan was on the very edge of surrender (as was known to U.S. officials), and that no American lives were saved by destroying the two cities.[6] But the dropping of the bombs had the important function of intimidating the Russians, toward which end several hundred thousand Japanese deaths were seen as a small price.

Since Hiroshima and Nagasaki, the United States has been alone in regularly brandishing atomic weapons, and on quite a few occasions it came very near to using them again.[7] The United States continues to refuse to renounce the first use of nuclear weapons in warfare. It has innovated continuously to make nuclear weapons tactically usable, and it has spawned a large intellectual and political constituency that strove for years to make nuclear war thinkable and a part of working military strategy.[8] In the Reagan years, proponents of the viability of nuclear war were an integral part of the policy planning apparatus. That administration, in talking up and planning to make nuclear war winnable, in its enormous nuclear arms buildup, its placement of cruise and Pershing missiles in Western Europe, and in its aggressive technological forward push, attempted to reestablish the nuclear superiority of the early postwar years. This would have allowed it to brandish the nuclear threat more credibly, thus permitting the freer use of the more standard modes of domination on a global basis. I would submit that this, in and of itself, is a major form of "terrorism."[9]

(2) *Sponsorship of Regime Terrorism.* Another very important form of terrorism used by the United States on a worldwide basis since 1945 has been the organization, sponsorship, and support of right-wing terrorist regimes. The breakup of the colonial empires and the revolutionary and democratic impulses accelerated by World War II posed a major threat to Western domination of the Third World. The United States stepped in to fill the gap. Under the guise of "containing" Soviet imperialism, the United States took on the role of propping up old regimes or replacing them with the neo-imperialist rule of compradors, military dictators, the free market, and the American Embassy. The policies formerly applicable to the "banana republics" of Central America were extended to the entire world, as the United States assumed global "responsibilities."

The primary functions of the new comprador and military leaderships was to preserve the main features of the old order, to maintain an open door and friendly climate for foreign investment, and to keep the countries as subordinates within the Free World alliance. Given the income and social inequalities of the old regimes, and the newly unleashed ideas of democracy and opportunity, the "new-old-order" installed by the United States required a massive dose of terror to keep the masses in the proper state of apathy. It also demanded tolerance of thievery on a gigantic scale, as the people (compradors and military officers) who were willing to serve as surrogates for a foreign power have been almost uniformly venal. In Guatemala, the Philippines, Argentina, Brazil, pre-Sandinista Nicaragua, Chile, Indonesia, and Zaire (among others), the elites put in power and supported by the West have been not merely brutal terrorists, but rapacious as well. Chomsky and I have referred to the countries they rule as "shakedown states."[10]

(3) *Direct Forms of Terrorism.* The United States has also used the more conventional forms of terrorism such as assassinations, sabotage, and the organization of armed bands and terrorist armies. The attacks on Cuba by the United States provide a remarkable case study in multi-dimensional state terror combined with the process of "transference" — that is, accusing Cuba of doing precisely what the United States was doing *to* Cuba. The record shows: eight *acknowledged* assassination attempts against Castro;[11] extensive sabotage of shipping, crops and animals, warehouse stores, terminals, oil facilities, and power stations; raids to disrupt activities and kill; and at one point the organization of an abortive proxy invasion.[12] The campaign of subversion "began virtually at the moment of revolutionary victory in 1959, stretched through the 1960s into the 1970s and endures, vestigially at least, to this day...."[13] After the failed Bay of Pigs invasion of 1961, the Kennedy administration organized a massive subversive effort under the code name "Operation Mongoose," which involved "continuous sabotage raids" and a major campaign of disinformation,[14] which regularly charged Cuban subversion at the very moment that the United States was engaged in a *real* and massive subversion operation against Cuba (and many other Latin American states).[15] The right-wing Cuban refugee terror network, which came into existence in large measure as a result of CIA training for anti-Cuba operations, continued long after 1961 as an apparatus of terror employed not only against Cuba but other enemies of "freedom."[16]

This U.S. secret war against Cuba was not unique. There is a long record of U.S.-sponsored armed bands and attacks on the countries of Eastern Europe, the Soviet Union, China, and the Indochinese states, among others.[17] The U.S. sponsorship of the contras follows a long tradition in Central America as well. Also in a long tradition has been the U.S. outcry about somebody else's "terrorism" coincident with a massive application of terrorism by the United States or one of its proxies.

The sponsorship of terrorist armies to invade Guatemala in 1954 (successful), and Cuba in 1961 (unsuccessful), and to destroy the Nicaraguan revolution by disruption and violence between 1981 and 1990 (largely successful), has had several other notable features. First, all three were cases of revolutions from below, with governments coming into power that addressed the basic needs of a formerly depressed and repressed majority.[18] This process of social democratization has been consistently horrifying and intolerable to the U.S. elite. That elite is happy only with elite rule and amenable clients. The threat of a "demonstration effect" of successful performance in the majority interest is also frightening. What if the masses in the other countries of the empire were to get the idea that they were not necessarily born to serve their masters? Second, in the case of Guatemala and Nicaragua, the new stress on the majority was combined with a level of political freedom and bourgeois democracy that have been rare in Central America. With the overthrow of Arbenz in Guatemala in 1954, pluralism and bourgeois democracy disappeared. The entire pattern demonstrates that U.S. "counter-terrorism" is antithetical to *political* as well as social democracy.[19]

Mechanisms of Support of State Terrorism

The United States has built up and aided the forces of state terrorism in four ways: by the protection and rehabilitation of the fascist cadres defeated in World War II, by outright or proxy invasions to install or protect terrorist clients, by subversion aiming at the overthrow of disfavored (often democratic) governments, and by "supplying repression" via financial aid, training, and arms supply to security forces and military dictators. Of these, invasions have been important but they are relatively familiar and obvious in character and I will not address them further in this chapter.

(1) *Rehabilitating Fascists.* During and immediately after World War II the United States busily and aggressively organized forces for the struggle against the Left. A central feature of this process was the protection and rehabilitation of fascists. There were show trials at Nuremberg and elsewhere, and some top leaders were executed, but at the very same time large numbers of fascists were being protected and positioned for Cold War service. Most of these were not scientists with scarce skills — they were mainly bureaucrats and army and intelligence personnel, many of them mass murderers. This was worldwide in scope: in Thailand, under U.S. influence, a military dictatorship was allowed to take power headed

by Phibum Songkram, who was (in the words of a former CIA analyst) "the first pro-Axis dictator to regain power after the war."[20] In Greece, the pre-war pro-Nazi forces were gradually pushed to the fore and installed in power by the British and the United States, who eventually consolidated that power by means of a savage counterinsurgency war.[21] The large-scale protection of Nazi and fascist activists and killers is now well established,[22] although the Western public has been spared the details. This protection included the extensive fabrication of documents and the hiding and spiriting away of fascist cadres. Many fascist killers were relocated in Latin America and played an important role in the development of the National Security States. Others were allowed to escape to Spain and Portugal, both countries befriended and protected by the United States and other members of the Free World.

The nominal denazification and general protection and rehabilitation of fascists provided a structural base for state terrorism in a variety of ways. In cases like Thailand and Greece, terror was an immediate instrument of the reinstalled fascists. Elsewhere in Western Europe the fascist cadres were positioned within the NATO framework to resume their traditional role in case the Left proved strong enough to really threaten to attain power. Greece in 1967 and Chile in 1973 were models of how terror states could be quickly brought into being under U.S. auspices in the face of liberal or radical challenges.

The rehabilitated fascist cadres have also served as a pool or reserve army of counterrevolutionary operatives for use both in Europe and the Third World. The recent disclosures regarding Operation Gladio in Western Europe, with secret arms depots and armies and paramilitary groups maintained outside the orbit of democratic control, have provided one more piece of evidence of the great scope of U.S. sponsorship of rightwing forces positioned to subvert and to protect against unwanted change. These and other rehabilitated cadres have served as leaders and soldiers in colonial wars (Angola, Algeria, Rhodesia, Vietnam), in building up fascist terrorist networks in Latin America, and as organizers of terror in Europe itself. Much of the terrorism in Italy was carried out by neofascists drawing inspiration and support from Gladio, P-2 and the intelligence services most closely linked to the CIA and NATO.[23]

(2) *Subversion.* Another major mechanism of U.S. support of state terror has been by means of subversion. I use the term to describe actions

taken to discredit and destabilize opposed governments, including the use of disinformation, economic pressure and harassment, manipulating the institutional environment of the victim by bribery and the discriminatory use of aid, and encouraging and supporting conspiracies and coups. The United States is so powerful that these devices are used, and hardly even remarked upon, against its larger allies, many economically and militarily virtually occupied countries, with large numbers of locals serving the interests of the great foreign power. At the time of the overthrow of the elected government of Brazil in 1964, for example, the United States was doing the following:[24] (i) it had bribed hundreds of local politicians in a scandal so great that a Parliamentary Commission was forced to investigate the matter;[25] (ii) it had numerous journalists on its payroll, subsidized newspapers and magazines, and for 90 days before the election even rented the editorial page of Rio de Janiero's evening newspaper; (iii) it funded Brazilian think-tanks that poured forth a flood of books and pamphlets dispensing conservative ideology and disinformation; (iv) a U.S. corporation, Time, Inc., illegally controlled the largest Brazilian TV station, and dispensed strong pro-coup propaganda; (v) the U.S. government-funded American Institute for Free Labor Development (AIFLD) worked to depoliticize and weaken the union movement, and actively supported the 1964 coup; (vi) U.S. officials encouraged the military establishment to oust the legal government, and the United States even had ships offshore as moral support for the leaders of the coup.

U.S. dissemination of propaganda and disinformation intended to destabilize, and plotting with conspirators to displace legal governments, is even more extensive in lesser client states.[26] I use Brazil as an illustration because it is the most powerful state in Latin America, despite which the United States manipulated and subverted its institutions, politicians and military leaders virtually without restraint.

U.S. subversion frequently involves the use of money to buy people off. The money is often in the form of loans or gifts that reward "friends" and allow them to pay off *their* friends and buy support at home.[27] The most remarkable form of subversion by buy-off is undoubtedly the employment of the AFL-CIO, through the AIFLD, as an instrument for bribing labor leaders in client states. Dispensing large sums, the AIFLD has co-opted hundreds of Third World union leaders, inducing them to stick to "bread-and-butter" unionism and eschew politics (especially left politics) and split away from the politicized unions. AIFLD has regularly helped put in place anticommunist and repressive regimes that have served well the needs of multinational corporations and U.S. foreign policy, but which have been rabidly antiunion. AIFLD, in short, is a literally "subversive" intruder into any state in which it is allowed to function.

Another striking form of subversion has been through the sponsorship of and intervention in foreign elections. The United States has developed the "demonstration election" as an interventionary device, organized in a state in the process of pacification and used to reassure the home populace that the U.S. intrusion is well received by the population under siege. The U.S. media have proven extremely gullible in accepting the validity of such elections, held under conditions of state terror and severe repression.[28] Beyond this, the United States has intervened aggressively in many other foreign elections via money, advice, and propaganda support purveyed secretly by the CIA and openly by the National Endowment for Democracy.[29] Such interventionary processes are taken as democratizing in the U.S. press, although they frequently drain democratic substance from democratic forms.[30]

(3) *Supplying Repression.* A further major mechanism for U.S. support of state terrorism has been the buildup, financing, arming, and training of Third World police, intelligence, and military personnel. This is in fact a *primary form of subversion,* in which a deliberate attempt is made to bribe and brainwash the principal armed groups within dependent societies and make them de facto servants of a foreign power. This has been done with a quite clearly subversive purpose: to increase the power of the armed forces, to manipulate them ideologically into serving as an anticommunist and antipopulist force, and to train them in counterinsurgency (CI) techniques that would also serve U.S. objectives.[31] While the policy had important antecedents, it went into a rapid growth phase after the triumph of Fidel Castro in 1959. It flourished in the 1960s with the development of CI doctrine and the notion of *preventive* CI.[32] We would prevent Castros and Ho Chi Minhs by putting in place anti-radical political and armed forces who would nip insurgencies in the bud.[33]

CI strategy was initially tied in with a reformist "hearts and minds" complement (such as the Alliance of Progress), but the reformist component has invariably been submerged by CI, for a number of reasons. One is that CI is inherently reactionary, as it rests on an attempt to take advantage of superior state force without regard to underlying issues or justice. It employs power and advanced technology in areas such as methods of interrogation, and applies them to poor people in revolt. With the "superior" races seeking submission of the inferior on the basis of force alone, this is a system in which escalating barbarity is "built-in." A second reason for the submergence of "reform" is that reformers are potential radicals, or are willing to tolerate the continued existence of radicals,[34] so that they are immediately suspect and have often been murdered in preventive CI practice. Third, CI doctrine with an antireformist bias follows from the primacy of anticommunism in U.S. ideology. Political risks in the United States are incurred by supporting reformers who seek independence, who do business with radical states, or who take radical action like land reform at the expense of U.S. interests. No penalties are associated with support of a murderous right-wing regime that remains within the Free World. A fourth factor is that the groups who are the natural allies of anti-radical strategies in the client states are reactionary and antireformist. Doing business with them may require tolerance of the liquidation of reform and reformers.

Finally, the U.S. military, economic, and political elites who are close to and implement Third World policies are also often reactionary,[35] and they invariably put serviceability to U.S. interests ahead of all other considerations. Thus, as a practical matter, fascists are preferred either on principle or for "pragmatic" reasons as a lesser evil. The United States also has the great advantage of having numerous liberals who can expound on the virtues of liberty and reformism with great eloquence, and pretend that these are operative values in U.S. policy toward the Third World, while their superiors and the armed services train and put into place people like Pinochet, Castello Branco, Massera and Viola, Castillo Armas and Rios Montt, and numerous others.[36]

The U.S. training and buildup of client police and armed forces has been historically unique in scope and scale. Between 1950 and 1979 U.S. military aid programs transferred a huge $107.3 billion in arms and ammunition to various U.S. clients, in addition to some $121 billion in arms sales. Between 1973 and 1980 the United States sold $66.8 billion in arms to Third World countries, including vast quantities of firearms, chemical munitions, helicopters, and other police gear useful in CI and repression.[37] Since 1950 the United States has trained over 500,000 military personnel from 85 countries in the U.S. Army School of the Americas in Panama and in several hundred other military schools and bases within the United States and abroad. Under police training programs that began in 1954 and terminated in 1975, over 7,500 police officers received regular training in U.S. schools, and over a million regular policemen were given training abroad. Large quantities of arms and equipment were also transferred to foreign police departments. A large investment was made in improving police and military communications systems in client states, oriented to CI efficiency and control of protests and other disorders. Training was provided in the design and manufacture of home-made bombs and assassination devices, which was put to practical use by regular and irregular forces in the National Security States.[38] Training in advanced "methods of interrogation" was also offered in U.S. programs, with dire consequences (as discussed below).

U.S. training has had a very substantial political content, one expert noting that it was "aimed less at military expertise than...at cultivation of internal political attitudes favorable to the United States."[39] It has focused heavily on the menace of Castro, the evils and omnipresence of communism, methods of CI, and the merits of foreign investment as the route to development. Political scientist Frederick Nunn has stated that "subject to United States military influence on anticommunism, the [Third World] professional army officer became hostile to any form of populism."[40] There is a large body of evidence that U.S. training has given not the slightest nod to democracy and human rights; instead, *it provided all the essential ingredients of National Security State ideology.* The rise of the National Security State (NSS) in the U.S. sphere of influence was not fortuitous. It was also facilitated by the massive flow of ex-Nazis from Europe to Latin America under U.S. protection.[41]

Terror Outcomes

As already suggested, the massive U.S. military aid and training programs, and other forms of support to states such as South Africa, had important consequences.

(1) *Military Takeovers and the Rise of the National Security States.* There were 18 military takeovers in Latin America between 1960 and 1968. These coups, which replaced 11 freely elected governments with military regimes, were a predictable result of the buildup and "education" of the Latin armed forces. Many were led by U.S. trainees, and most of them were supported by the United States. The key Brazilian coup, for example, was led by the so-called "Sorbonne group," closest to the United States in personal affiliation and training background.[42] The Brazilian coup plans were known in advance by U.S. officials (who, of course, never warned the legally elected government), and the coup itself was greeted enthusiastically by the Kennedy liberals in Washington. (A classic remark by U.S. Ambassador to Brazil Lincoln Gordon was that the Brazilian coup was "the single most decisive victory for freedom in the mid-twentieth century.")[43] These attitudes were not exceptional, as evidenced by the fact that U.S. aid has moved fairly consistently in an inverse relationship to democratic and human rights conditions. In Table 1 we can see that as democratic conditions deteriorate (column 2, minus sign) there is a distinct tendency for total U.S. aid and multinational credits to increase markedly. In a more elaborate quantitative analysis of this relationship, Lars Schoultz found that the correlations between U.S. aid and human rights violations "are uniformly positive."[44] That is, the worse the human rights conditions, the greater the aid.

One can also see on Table 1 that as human rights conditions deteriorate, factors affecting the "climate of investment," like tax laws and labor repression, improve from the viewpoint of the multinational corporation. This suggests an important line of causation. Military dictatorships tend to improve the investment climate, and the multinational corporate community, and the U.S. government, are very sensitive to this factor. Military dictators enter into a tacit joint venture arrangement with Free World leaders: they will keep the masses quiet, maintain an open door to multinational investment, and provide bases and otherwise serve as loyal clients. In exchange, they will be aided and protected against their own people, and allowed to loot public property. Marcos was loyally supported by the United States for more than a decade on this reciprocal basis. The U.S. distancing in 1986 clearly had nothing to do with Marcos' longstanding fundamental behavior patterns. It is just that he had ceased to be able to keep the popula-

TABLE 1

U.S. Aid, Investment Climate, and Human Rights in Ten Countries

Country	Strategic Political Dates[1] (1)	Positive (+) or Negative (−) Effects on Democracy (2)	(−) Means an increased use of torture or death squads (3)	(−) Means an increase in no. of political prisoners (4)	Improvement in Investment Climate: Tax Laws Eased (+) (5a)	Improvement in Investment Climate: Labor Repressed (+) (5b)	Economic Aid (% change)[2] (6)	Military Aid (% change) (7)	(6) + (7) (% change) (8)	U.S. and Multinational Credits (% change) (9)	Total Aid (8) + (9) (% change) (10)
Brazil	1964	−	−	−	+	+	+ 14	− 40	− 7	+ 180	+ 112
Chile	1973	−	−	−	+	+	+ 558	− 8	+ 259	+ 1,079	+ 770
Dominican Republic	1965	−	−	NA	+	+	+ 57	+ 10	+ 52	+ 305	+ 133
Guatemala	1954	−	−	NA	+	+	NA	NA	NA	NA	+ 5,300
Indonesia	1965	−	−	−	+	NA	− 81	− 79	− 81	+ 653	+ 62
Iran	1953	−	−	−	+	+	NA	NA	NA	NA	+ 900
Philippines	1972	−	−	−	+	+	+ 204	+ 67	+ 143	+ 171	+ 161
South Korea	1972	−	−	−	+	+	− 52	− 56	− 55	+ 183	− 9
Thailand	1973	+	+	NA	−	−	− 63	− 64	− 64	+ 218	+ 5
Uruguay	1973	−	−	−	+	+	− 11	+ 9	− 2	+ 32	+ 21

Sources:
1. Information on torture and political prisoners mostly from the *Amnesty International Report on Torture*, 1975 and *The Amnesty International Report, 1975-76, &1976*; supplemented with data from newspaper articles, journals, and books on the specific countries. Data on investment climate largely from articles, journals, and books on the specific countries.
2. Data on aid taken from *U.S. Overseas Loans and Grants and Assistance from International Organizations*, A.I.D., 1972 and 1976 editions, for years 1962-1975. Data previous to 1962 taken from *Historical Statistics of the United States*, Bicentennial Edition, Dept. of Commerce, 1975.

TABLE 2

U.S. Military, Police and Economic Aid to Countries Using Torture on an Administrative Basis in the 1970s[1] (Figures in Millions of Dollars)

Country	Military Assistance[2] (1946-1979)	Commercial Arms Exports[3] (1950-1980)	No. of Military Personnel Trained by U.S.[4] (1950-1980)	Police Aid[5] (1973-1981)	Bilateral U.S. Economic Aid[6] (1946-1979)	International Aid[7] (1946-1980)
Argentina*	263.6	90.4	4,017	0.45	199.1	2,946.7
Bolivia	80.7	4.28	4,896	15.78	801.8	1,027.2
Brazil	640.0	83.31	8,659	0.77	2,424.1	9,080.6
Chile	217.0	8.76	6,883	0.14	1,163.1	1,046.6
Colombia	240.9	19.40	8,349	34.17	1,340.7	4,095.6
Dominican Republic	43.0	2.59	4,269	-	589.4	733.9
Guatemala	41.5	5.09	3,334	-	417.4	703.5
Haiti	5.9	1.87	643	-	251.8	305.0
Mexico	0.1	12.97	1,003	95.1	2,691.9	5,807.3
Nicaragua	32.4	4.24	5,673	-	298.9	537.1
Peru	239.7	25.63	8,160	8.4	609.3	1,434.1
Paraguay	30.3	2.45	2,018	0.09	177.8	629.1
Uruguay	89.2	1.67	2,806	-	159.5	632.3
Venezuela*	152.3	60.33	5,540	-	201.1	657.0

1. For the concept and criteria of torture on an administrative basis, see Chomsky and Herman, *The Washington Connection and Third World Fascism*, frontispiece and explanatory footnotes.
2. Agency for International Development, Congressional Presentation, Fiscal Year 1982, Annex III (3), Latin America and the Caribbean.
3. U.S. Department of Defense, Congressional Presentation, Security Assistance Programs, Fiscal Year 1982.
4. Ibid.
5. Michael Klare and Cynthia Arnson, *Supplying Repression*, IPS, 1981, p. 3. This column refers to police aid provided for a brief period under the International Narcotics Control Program. The much larger Public Safety Program supplied $324 million of arms and training to Third World police between 1961 and 1973 (ibid., p. 21).
6. See footnote 2.
7. Ibid.
* The data source for both Argentina and Venezuela, for military assistance, bilateral, and international economic aid categories was: US A.I.D., US Overseas Loans and Grants...July 1, 1945-September 30, 1979.

Reproduced from Herman, *The Real Terror Network*, p. 129.

tion quiet any longer, which was an important part of the bargain. Thus, suddenly, at this point, the U.S. media discovered that he steals and was not a good democrat.

(2) *U.S. Aid and the Growth of Torture.* Torture has had what Amnesty International calls "a cancerous growth" in recent decades. After the death of Stalin in 1953 it declined markedly in the East. It has been a growth industry in the West. What is more, this terrible and dehumanizing form of violence is almost exclusively an instrument of *state* terror.[45] That it should have grown dramatically as an instrument of state terror while the new concern over something called "terror" was restricted to non-state terror, reinforces the point that the powerful define terrorism to their own advantage and independently of the substance of terror.

Table 2 shows the relationship between U.S. aid and training for 15 countries using torture on an administrative basis in the 1970s. A more comprehensive overview shows that of 35 countries using systematic torture in the 1970s, 26 (or 74%) were clients of the United States.[46] While I have not updated these results in detail, despite the ebbs and flows of the past decade I do not think that there have been any major changes in pattern.[47]

The linkage between U.S. aid and the use of torture is not coincidental. We have seen that the installation and support of repressive regimes has been functional. The United States is also wealthy, and can provide its clients with the best and latest in methods and tools of interrogation. There is a great deal of evidence of U.S. training in methods of torture and provision of torture technology, which have been diffused throughout the system of U.S. client states. Electronic methods of torture, used extensively in Vietnam, have been adapted throughout the U.S. sphere of influence. A.J. Langguth claims that the CIA advised the Brazilian military on the limits that would prevent premature death in the use of field telephones for interrogation.[48] A recently published interview with a Salvadoran death squad officer shows that officials from the Salvadoran police and intelligence services have received intensive training in interrogation methods from the United States, including advice on the use of torture.[49]

The U.S. official position has always been that U.S. police training stresses "humane" methods of interrogation, as well as greater police efficiency, but there has been a remarkable correlation between the coming of such training and the emergence of death squads and the rise of systematic torture. In 1985 U.S. Congressman George Miller released a May 19, 1970 Airgram from the U.S. Embassy in Guatemala to the State Department reporting on the torture and assassination activities of a Guatemalan death squad made up of security personnel. Scrawled on the top of the first page of this document from an unnamed Foreign Service officer was the statement: "Jack — This is what we were afraid of with increased public safety support."[50]

In its *Report on Torture*, Amnesty International noted that torture came to Greece with the 1967 coup of the Colonels, whose leaders were trained and supported by the CIA and U.S. Army. AI points out that the United States regularly apologized for the torture regime, because it liked what it was doing in general.[51] AI noted a "seeming paradox" — that "never has there been a stronger or more universal consensus on the total inadmissibility of the practice of torture: at the same time the practice of torture has reached epidemic proportions."[52] The solution to the paradox is simple: terrorism, as we have seen, is defined in accordance with the requirements of power. Just as power permits the exclusion of South Africa and Guatemala from the category of "terrorist states," so that same power may exclude countries using institutionalized torture from the list of terrorist states and their practices from the consciousness of Western publics. The premier terrorist as portrayed in the U.S. media during the period of the worst excesses of the Argentinian regime of organized torture (1976-83)[53] was *Libya*. Argentina was a slightly troublesome friend, not a terrorist state.[54]

(3) *U.S. Aid and Training and the Spread of the Death Squad and "Disappearances."* Latin America has been unique in world politics in recent decades in developing an institution called the "death squad" and in the recrudescence of the phenomenon of "disappearances." The death squad is a sub rosa group of killers, who abduct enemies of the state and frequently torture and kill them and cause them to "disappear." Their function is to kill and intimidate without attribution to the official forces of the state. U.S. officials generally accept the claims of the client states that the "death squads" are unconnected with the state, as this allows them to rationalize support for the state committing the organized murders. The

TABLE 3

The Origin and Spread of the Death Squad in Latin America*

Country	Death Squad Organization	U.S. Role in Introduction of Responsible Government	U.S. Police Training	Numbers of U.S.-Trained Military Personnel 1950-1975	U.S. Military Aid 1946-1980 ($million)
Argentina	1973[1]	Acquiescent	Extensive	4,017	263.6
Bolivia	Late 1970s	"	"	4,896	80.7
Brazil	1964	Major	"	8,659	640.0
Chile	1973	"	"	6,883	217.0
Dominican Republic	1965	"	"	4,269	43.0
El Salvador	1963-66[2]	Acquiescent[3]	"	2,097	5.0
Guatemala	1966-67	Major	"	3,334	41.5
Mexico	Early 1970s	Not applicable (government of long standing)	"	1,003	0.1
Nicaragua	Early 1970s	Major	"	5,673	32.4
Uruguay	1968-70	Acquiescent	"	2,806	89.2

* This table is confined to countries in which semi-official death squads were well established—in still others there were unexplained political murders and disappearances of dissenters, and systematic torture. Sources for this compilation are: Amnesty International, *Report on Torture* (1975), *'Disappearances'* (1980), *Testimony on Secret Detention Camps in Argentina* (1980); *Guatemala, A Government Program of Political Murder* (1981), and other AI country reports on the relevant states; the books by Black, Langguth and Lernoux cited in the text and footnotes; Norman Gall "Slaughter in Guatemala" and "Santo Domingo: The Politics of Terror," *New York Review of Books*, May 20, 1970 and July 22, 1971; Argentine Information Service Committee, *Argentina Today, A Dossier on Repression and the Violation of Human Rights* (1976); NACLA, *El Salvador* (2 parts, March-April and July-August 1980); on Mexico, see releases of the Council on Hemispheric Affairs on Human Rights dated February 3, 1979 and June 8, 1981; AID, *U.S. Overseas Loans and Grants* (1976 ed.); NACLA, "The Pentagon's Proteges, U.S. Training Programs for Foreign Military Personnel," (Janurary 1976); Michael T. Klare and Cynthia Arnson, *Supplying Repression*, Institute for Policy Studies, 1981, p. 5.
1. Death squads and systematic torture originated in the Eva Peron era of declining constitutional government—they increased sharply in importance after the military coup of March 1976.
2. Orden, a para-military network of spies, informers and enforcers was founded by General Medano in the mid-1960s to combat "subversion." One of its functions was to "handle 'disappearances' of community leaders." Lernoux, *Cry of the People*, p. 72.
3. On the Kennedy administration's support of the military government of Col. Rivera, and the 1972 U.S. support of massive election fraud and a still more repressive military regime (helped along by Nicaragua and Guatemala), see NACLA, "El Salvador—Why Revolution?," *Report on the Americas*, March-April 1980, pp. 13-17.

Table reproduced from Herman, *The Real Terror Network*, p. 116.

claim is ludicrous — the evidence is clear that the death squads are usually made up of off-duty and irregular official forces and are under the control of the state[55] — but the acceptance of these claims by U.S. officials shows the essentially collective and supportive relations between the United States and clients employing this mode of terror.

The death squad spread throughout Latin America in the 1960s and 1970s. It was terminated in Nicaragua with the Sandinista triumph, and was ended or greatly reduced in Argentina, Brazil, and Uruguay as a result of the recession in military rule in those states. It is still important to recognize that it became very widespread in the U.S. sphere of influence, and that its rapid growth was closely correlated with U.S. aid and training (see Table 3). The death squad emerged in the Dominican Republic immediately after the U.S. invasion and intensified training of 1965-66. It emerged in Brazil immediately after the U.S.-sponsored 1964 coup. It came to Guatemala after the reestablishment of close U.S. hegemony in 1954, and especially after the influx of Green Berets and CI training in 1966-67.

"Disappearances" have been a continent-wide phenomenon in Latin America. This horrendous development has brought forth groups of relatives of the victims in over a dozen Latin American states, who have held a series of Conferences of Relatives of the Disappeared each year since 1981. (These conferences have been essentially ignored in the Free World press.) It is estimated that the number of disappeared persons in Latin America since 1960 now exceeds 100,000, including over 35,000 Guatemalans alone. There is a close correlation between death squad activity and disappearances, and between U.S. aid and training and disappearances as well.

It should be noted that the decline in death squad activity and disappearances in countries like Argentina, Brazil and Uruguay was in no way attributable to U.S. policy or pressures — it came, in fact, from the catastrophic failures of the U.S.-supported military regimes and their inability to retain open power.[56] In an area of intense ongoing U.S. interest and activity, like Central America in the 1980s, the death squad and disappearances took on new life. In El Salvador, for example, the enlarged U.S. interest beginning in 1979 led to a huge surge in death squad and regular army killing of civilians. Honduras, increasingly occupied by the United States in the 1980s, quickly joined the list of countries subjected to disappearances.[57]

TABLE 4

The U.S. Assault on Socialism

Forms of Aggression	Victim Countries*													
	USSR	China	North Korea	Vietnam	Cambodia	Laos	Cuba	Angola	Grenada	E.Europe	Nicaragua*	Dominican Republic*	Guatemala*	Libya*
1. Direct invasion or air attack	+		+	+	+	+			+			+		+
2. Indirect (proxy) invasion		+					+	+					+	
3. Threat of atomic bombing	+		+	+										
4. Sponsoring armies & terrorists on borders	+	+		+	+		+	+		+	+			
5. Sabotage raids	+	+		+			+	+		+	+			
6. Attempted assassination of high officials		+	+				+			+	+			+
7. Boycotts	+	+	+	+	+	+	+	+	+	+	+		+	+
8. Deliberate imposition of arms costs	+										+			

*Not all of these countries are or were "socialist"; Guatemala in 1954 and Nicaragua in the 1980s were social democracies threatening a positive demonstration effect; the

(4) *Escalated "Surrogate" Terrorism.* One of the purposes of U.S. sponsorship of right-wing and counterrevolutionary states, and training of security forces within states, has been to establish surrogates, who could function as regional gendarmes. The Shah of Iran and Israel in the Middle East, South Africa and France in Africa, Brazil in Latin America, have been notable instruments of the surrogate strategy. Some have fallen by the wayside, but the strategy is very much alive and new candidates will be mobilized in the future, even though the United States is positioning itself more and more for "open" covert action and direct attack under the guise of "counter-terrorism." Under Reagan, the violence of the surrogates escalated markedly, as discussed elsewhere in this book. The suffering produced by surrogate state terror has vastly exceeded that inflicted by those designated in the West as terrorists, who kill on a smaller scale and do not regularly torture their victims.

(5) *Effective Damaging or Destruction of the Progress of Social Democracy and Socialism.* The failures of socialism in the world have no doubt been a result in good part of bureaucratic excesses, centralization, and a crucial failure to fulfil the best ideals of socialism as a system of participatory democracy. But a large although unmeasurable contributor to these failures was incessant U.S. and Western hostility and attack, from 1917 onward. These attacks on what were already poor and struggling countries, permitted them no breathing room and, by posing ongoing military threats, encouraged authoritarian reactions and forced mobilizations. Promising forms of democratic mobilization, as in Guatemala, Chile and Nicaragua, were terminated by U.S.-organized terror. A good case can be made that socialism never had a chance in instances where it showed promise, as a result of Western-organized hostility and violence.

Table 4 represents a preliminary effort to identify the different forms of Western-organized attacks on countries deemed a threat to Western interests. A number of these were not socialist (Iran in the Mossadegh era, Chile, the Dominican Republic, Nicaragua) but were controlled by reformers or radicals whose programs were offensive to Western planners. Even these could not be permitted to survive. The West aggressively attempted to "bury" social democracy as well as socialism by hostile and violent tactics from time immemorial.

The Old and New Orders

The Western view is that if Libya or the Soviet Union train and give (or sell) guns to somebody, they are accountable for the behavior of their trainees or buyers of their weapons. As usual, this reasoning is not applied symmetrically. The United States has been the greatest trainer and supplier of arms in world history, and the acceleration of its activity as trainer-supplier in the 1960s and 1970s was associated with the emergence of an extensive network of military dictatorships and National Security States. The growth of torture and disappearances was largely attributable to the workings of this *real* terror network, and in the 1980s the mass slaughters of major U.S. surrogates — Israel and South Africa — were major contributors to quantitatively substantial world terrorism. The escalation of U.S. intervention in Central America, notably in sponsoring the *contras* and the "death squad democracy" of El Salvador, has also made a major contribution to terrorist violence.

The coming into power of the Reagan administration was also associated with a huge arms buildup and attempt to make the nuclear threat more credible and nuclear war winnable. This was an important form of terrorism in itself; but its main function was to make it easier for the United States and its surrogates to employ conventional forces and to support "freedom fighters" like Savimbi in Angola and the Nicaraguan *contras* on a world-wide basis. The Big Lies that covered over the Reagan policies of unconstrained arms escalation and counterrevolution — in the names of "counter-terrorism" and "freedom" — were effective, and Western publics were made confused, fearful, and thus manageable. The Bush years witnessed the collapse of the Soviet bloc and a more aggressive U.S. projection of power abroad. The first major international intervention that followed the end of the Cold War was the U.S. invasion of Panama in December 1989. The Gulf War, little more than a year later, allowed the United States to smash a somewhat independent Middle East power, firm up control of some of its most important oil dependencies and reassert the role of the military and the security state. The great political success of the Gulf War for George Bush points ominously toward external aggression and "police" actions as the effective mode of bailout of U.S. political leaders performing poorly at home. This suggests a continuation and possible intensification of the Reagan era pattern of direct terrorist attacks and sponsorship of terrorist states and "freedom fighters" abroad. With the "Soviet threat" (i.e., a countervailing great power) out of the way, the pacification of the Third World should run more smoothly in the near future.

In *The Real Terror Network,* written in 1981, I pointed out that Reagan's policies would not only greatly enlarge state terrorism, his parochial and repressive policies at home and abroad and refusal to address real problems would generate more terrorism from below (retail terrorism). "This natural result of greed, short-sightedness and stupidity will then be used to justify greater state violence, which will be wrapped up in an 'antiterrorist' flag. Right-wing ideologues create retail terrorists and are then quite prepared to kill them"(p. 213). This is the ultimate Orwellism: those who terrorize the most are able to take the puny responses of their victims and use these to justify their own further excesses. It is a feedback system that can only be fought by a determined effort to understand the reality, to call it by its right names, and to organize to contest the hegemony of the dominant terrorists.

Notes

1. Joseph Hanlon, *Beggar Your Neighbors,* London: Catholic Institute for International Relations, 1986; Phyllis Johnson and David Martin, *Frontline Southern Africa: Destructive Engagement,* New York: Four Walls Eight Windows, 1988.
2. See Richard Leonard, *South Africa at War,* Westport, Conn.: Lawrence Hill, 1983.
3. Gadhafi talks big, but carries a small terrorist stick. The U.S. leadership, by contrast, talks "anti-terrorism" and "counter-terrorism," but carries a gigantic terrorist stick. See Table 1 and the text below.
4. See Edward S. Herman and Gerry O'Sullivan, *The "Terrorism" Industry: The Experts and Institutions That Shape Our View of Terror,* New York: Pantheon Books, 1990, chap. 3, "The Western Model of Terror."
5. Both Guatemala and El Salvador have been receiving aid from the United States under "anti-terrorism" programs. See ibid., pp. xiii-xiv.
6. See Robert L. Messer, "New evidence on Truman's decision," *Bulletin of Atomic Scientists,* August 1985, pp. 50-56 for a good review and citations. Characteristically, President Truman lied in stating on the occasion of the Hiroshima bombing that the attack had been made on a military site.
7. As Dan Ellsberg has said: "The notion common to nearly all Americans that 'no nuclear weapons have been used since Nagasaki' is mistaken....Again and again, generally in secret from the American public, U.S. nuclear weapons *have* been used, for quite different purposes: in the precise way that a gun is used when you point it at someone's head in a direct confrontation, whether or not the trigger is pulled."

"Introduction" to E.P. Thompson and Dan Smith, eds., *Protest and Survive*, New York: Monthly Review Press, 1981, p. i. Ellsberg goes on to describe a substantial number of cases in which the U.S. threatened to use nuclear weapons.

8. Fred Kaplan, *The Wizards of Armegeddon*, New York: Simon and Schuster, 1983; Robert Scheer, *With Enough Shovels: Reagan, Bush & Nuclear War*, New York: Random House, 1982.
9. This is stressed in William D. Perdue, *Terrorism and the State: A Critique of Domination Through Fear*, New York: Praeger, 1989, Chap. 4.
10. *The Washington Connection and Third World Fascism*, Montréal, Black Rose Books, 1979 pp. 61-66.
11. *Alleged Assassination Plots Involving Foreign Leaders*, Rep. No. 94-465, Select Committee to Study Government Intelligence Activities, U.S. Senate, 84th Cong., 1st Sess, Nov. 1975, pp. 75ff.
12. For many details on all of these efforts, see Warren Hinckle and William Turner, *The Fish Is Red: The Story of The Secret War Against Castro*, New York: Harper and Row, 1981.
13. Ibid., p. vii.
14. "All major CIA stations abroad assigned at least one case officer full time to gathering intelligence, trying to turn the host country against Cuba, and encouraging the defection of Cuban officials. Reports from this far-flung network were funneled to the Miami station for correlation and action." Ibid., p. 113.
15. For many examples, see Philip Agee *Inside the Company: CIA Diary*, New York: Bantam, 1976.
16. Edward S. Herman, *The Real Terror Network: Terrorism in Fact and Propaganda*, Montréal, Black Rose Books, 1982, pp. 65-69.
17. John Loftus, *The Belarus Secret*, Harmondsworth, Middlesex, England: Penguin, 1983, passim.; Victor Marchetti and John D. Marks, *The CIA and the Cult of Intelligence*, New York: Dell, 1980, Chapter 4 ["Special Operations"].
18. One group of Central American experts speaks of the Sandinista aims as follows: "The FSLN sought to fill the political and institutional vacuum by creating new political structures that responded to its agenda of social transformation. The agenda defined national priorities according to 'the logic of the majority,' which meant that Nicaragua's poor majority would have access to, and be the primary beneficiaries of, public programs." *Report of the Latin American Studies Association Delegation to Observe the Nicaraguan General Election of November 4*, 1984, pp. 4-5.
19. This is spelled out in detail in Edward S. Herman, "The United States versus Human Rights in the Third World," *Harvard Human Rights Journal*, Spring 1991, pp. 98-103.
20. Frank Darling, *Thailand and the United States*, Washington, D.C.: Public Affairs Press, 1965, p. 65.
21. Lawrence S. Wittner, *American Intervention in Greece, 1941-1949*, New York: Columbia University Press, 1982, Chapter 8 ["The Military Solution"]
22. See "Special: Nazis, the Vatican, and CIA," special issue of *Covert Action Information Bulletin*, Number 25, Winter 1986, esp. Peter Dale Scott, "How Allen Dulles and the SS Preserved Each Other"; also, Magnus Linklater, Isabel Hinton and Neal Ascherson, *The Fourth Reich: Klaus Barbie and the Neo-Fascist Connection*, London: Hodder and Stoughton, 1984; Christopher Simpson, *Blowback: America's Recruitment of Nazis and Its Effect on the Cold War*, New York: Weidenfeld & Nicolson, 1988, passim; Noam Chomsky, *Turning the Tide*, Montreal: Black Rose Books, 1983. pp. 194-202.
23. Edward S. Herman and Frank Brodhead, *The Rise and Fall of the Bulgarian Connection*, New York: Sheridan Square Publications, 1986, Chapter 4 ["The Rome-Washington

Connection II']; Gianni Flamini, *Il partito del golpe: Le strategie della tensione e de terrore dal primo centrosinistra organico al sequestro Moro*, vol. I, Ferrara, Italo Bovolenta, 1981, Chapter 1.

24. See Jan K. Black, *United States Penetration of Brazil*, Philadelphia: University of Pennsylvania Press, 1977, esp. Part II.
25. The Commission's work was, of course, ended following the coup. Ibid, p. 73.
26. Several dramatic illustrations are given, with extensive details, in Philip Agee, *Inside the Company: CIA Diary*, New York: Bantam, 1976.
27. Just prior to the Italian elections of April 1948, the U.S. Congress voted a special Marshall Plan subsidy of $227 million for Italy, much of it transmitted secretly to the Christian Democratic Party and split-off trade unions organized under U.S. sponsorship. See Roberto Faenza and Marco Fini, *Gli americani in Italia*, Milan: Feltrinelli, 1976, p. 298. Vast sums in U.S. gifts and loans, and loans from organizations like the World Bank, have gone to U.S. friends like Suharto and Marcos, despite clear evidence of a huge corruption drain. The services rendered by these friends have been substantial, however. See text below on the implicit trade-offs.
28. See Edward S. Herman and Frank Brodhead, *Demonstration Elections: U.S.-Staged elections in the Dominican Republic, Viet Nam and El Salvador*, Boston: South End Press, 1984.
29. *National Endowment for Democracy (NED): A Foreign Policy Branch Gone Awry*, A Report of the Council on Hemispheric Affairs and Inter-Hemispheric Education Resource Centre, Albuquerque, NM, March 1990.
30. See Herman, "The United States versus Human Rights in the Third World," pp. 98-103.
31. See ibid., pp. 86-90 for documentation.
32. See Michael McClintock, *The American Connection: State Terror and Popular Resistance in El Salvador*, vol. I, London: Zed Press, 1985, Part 1 ["The U.S. and the Doctrine of Counter-Insurgency"].
33. This was the language used in a speech on "The U.S. Role in Stability Operations," included as a standard speech in a "Speechmake Kit" used by the army in the late 1960s. Upheavals from below "can be controlled if we are successful in nipping every Communist insurgency in the bud. This is what we hope to do." Quoted by J. W. Fulbright, *The Pentagon Propaganda Machine*, New York: Liveright, 1970, p. 82.
34. One of Juan Bosch's critical failings from the standpoint of the Kennedy liberals was his unwillingness to deport or otherwise persecute Communists, which was viewed as a sign of his lack of fealty to higher Free World principles. See Piero Gliejeses, *The Dominican Crisis*, Baltimore: Johns Hopkins, 1978, pp. 87-89.
35. This is why the U.S. training programs have made U.S. trainees more reactionary and undemocratic than previously; it also explains the extreme protectiveness of U.S. Embassies and officials of client terrorists. For a discussion of both these points, see Herman, "The United States versus Human Rights in the Third World," pp. 88-96.
36. Given the political costs of a Communist assumption of power in a client state, and the fact that most liberals have also internalized the primacy of anticommunism, the policies of liberals who achieve power are often indistinguishable from those of the reactionaries. Johnson and his associates fought desperately to keep the social democrat Juan Bosch out of power in the Dominican Republic. The Kennedy liberals were enthused at the military coup in Brazil and displacement of a social democratic government. A major spurt in the growth of National Security States in Latin America took place under Kennedy and Johnson.

37. Michael Klare and Cynthia Arnson, *Supplying Repression,* Washington, Institute for Policy Studies, 1981, pp. 44-45; Michael Klare, *American Arms Supermarket,* Austin: University of Texas Press, 1984, p. 9. Based on export licenses issued for sales to Third World police alone — excluding the larger volumes sold to armies and paramilitary groups — Michael Klare found that between September 1976 and May 1979, U.S. firms supplied the following: 615,612 gas grenades, 126,622 revolvers, 51,906 rifles and machine guns, 12,605 canisters of chemical mace, and 56 million rounds of ammunition. Ibid., p. 191.
38. See Herman, *The Real Terror Network,* pp. 128-31; Klare and Arnson, *Supplying Repression,* p. 6.
39. Dr. R. K. Baker, quoted in Miles Wolpin, *Military Aid and Counterrevolution in the Third World,* Boston: Lexington, 1972, p. 31
40. Quoted in Jan Black, op. cit., p. 194.
41. See note 22 above.
42. See Black, op. cit., pp. 176-78.
43. Quoted in ibid., p. 55.
44. "U.S. Foreign Policy and Human Rights Violations in Latin America: A Comparative Analysis of Foreign Aid Distributions," *Comparative Politics,* Jan. 1981, p. 162.
45. "Torture today is essentially a state activity." Amnesty International, *Report on Torture,* p. 22.
46. See Chomsky and Herman, *The Washington Connection,* frontispiece and notes. Parent-client relationship was based primarily on receipt of military training and significant flows of direct economic and military aid. For more details, and the criteria used in determining countries using torture on an administrative basis, see p. 361.
47. See Amnesty International, *Torture in the 1980s,* New York: AI, 1984.
48. *Hidden Terrors,* New York: Pantheon, 1978, p. 139. This book gives substantial evidence of U.S. training in and support of torture in a number of Latin American states.
49. Allan Nairn, "Confessions of a Death Squad Officer," *The Progressive,* March 1986, p. 28.
50. Quoted in Kai Bird and Max Holland, "Capitol Letter," *The Nation,* Dec. 14, 1985.
51. *Report on Torture,* New York: Farrar, Straus and Giroux, 1975, p. 81.
52. Ibid., p. 31.
53. At its peak, Argentina had at least 60 separate detention centers in which torture was regularly employed. See Amnesty International, *Testimony on secret detention camps in Argentina,* New York: AI, 1980.
54. On the modes of apologetics and evasions on Argentina in the U.S. press, see Chomsky and Herman, *The Washington Connection,* pp. 263-70.
55. See esp. Amnesty International, *'Disappearances': A Workbook,* New York: AI, 1981, chap. 8.
56. See Edward S. Herman and James Petras, "'Resurgent Democracy' In Latin America: Myth and Reality," *New Left Review,* Number 154, Nov.-Dec. 1985.
57. Estimates of disappearances in Honduras ranging from 147-200 are given in "Human Rights Watch," *Latinamerican Press,* March 17, 1986, and James LeMoyne, "CIA Accused of Tolerating Killings in Honduras," *New York Times,* February 14, 1986.

Chapter Two

Beyond Rollback: U.S. Foreign Policy Into the 1990s[*]

Robert Gould and Thomas Bodenheimer

What has happened in the last two glorious weeks in the U.S.S.R. is...cause for special celebration among American conservatives who brought about the pivotal historical event that led to Soviet Communism's demise: the election of Ronald Reagan in 1980.

Unlike the days of Gerald Ford and Jimmy Carter, when the Soviets were blithely gobbling up countries in Indochina, East Asia, Africa, and Central America, Ronald Reagan not only halted communism's seemingly endless advances, but achieved what no other President had done before him: *He significantly rolled back the Soviet empire....*

Through his determination to supply arms to anti-Communist insurgent forces, rebuild our military with Stealths, B-1 bombers, advanced missiles and a 600-ship Navy, place Pershing IIs and cruise missiles into Europe and push for a weapons system that obviously still frightens the Soviets — the Strategic Defense Initiative — Ronald Reagan clearly forced the Soviets to change direction under Gorbachev.

---

[*] This chapter is based on the authors' book *Rollback!: Right-wing Power in U.S. Foreign Policy.* Boston: South End Press, 1989.

Sensing that he was willing to cry "Uncle" in his economic and military battle against the West, Reagan seized the initiative by agreeing to work with the new Soviet leader...to allow him to stage a major global retreat. With relatively little loss of blood, that retreat has ended in the rout of communism worldwide.[1]

As trumpeted in a recent front page article of the U.S. national conservative weekly *Human Events*, the total defeat of the U.S.S.R., the ultimate aim of U.S. foreign policy since the dawn of the Cold War, is now an undisputed fact. This chapter will attempt to analyze how the world-historical collapse of Soviet power has been influenced by the aggressive interweaving of two often contentious expressions of anti-communism within the U.S. ruling establishment — those forces historically calling for *containment* of the Soviet Union and its allies, versus those who all along advocated the more overtly aggressive strategy of *rollback*. We will also examine the impact of these clashing and synergistic world-views on the U.S. response to the rapidly unfolding post-Soviet landscape.

Traditional Conservatives and Containment

Since the ascension of the United States to world power status in the first decades of this century, through the dawn of the Cold War, the conduct of foreign policy had generally been considered the province of the "traditional conservative" elites who have represented internationally-minded economic interests in the United States. This "Eastern Establishment" of large multinational industries and banks provided business support for the New Deal, and favoured free-trade. In the 1930s this bloc, with such companies as Chase Manhattan Bank, Standard Oil, General Electric, IBM and many others, supported internationalism rather than isolationism abroad, with a strong European orientation.

It was through its most important foreign policy organ, the Council on Foreign Relations, that conservative business planned the entire post-war conception of a U.S.-dominated world order. With the decimation of the European and Japanese colonial powers resulting from World War II, the United States was poised to assert domination over the former colonial domains while aiming to reconstitute the former centres of capitalism, under the rubric of "Pax Americana."[2]

Prior to World War II, the traditional elites had been vigorously anti-Soviet, as illustrated by the diplomatic history ranging from the time anti-Bolshevik expeditionary forces were sent to intervene in the Russian Civil War. With post-war Europe prostrate before a victorious Red Army that the United States could not yet deliver enough nuclear weapons against, *realpolitik* dictated an elite strategy that avoided a direct military *rollback* of the U.S.S.R. Instead, policy makers aimed at the *containment* of Soviet power and influence in the world, within an overall atmosphere of global stability and trade, based largely on the exercise of economic or political clout. However, as George Kennan would argue in his famous "Sources of Soviet Conduct" article, such clout was to be applied forcefully:

> ...But the United States has it in its power to increase enormously the strains under which Soviet policy must operate...and in this way to promote tendencies which must eventually find their outlet in either the break-up or the gradual mellowing of Soviet power.[3]

Paul Nitze, an investment banker with ties to military contractors authored policy document NSC-68, which provided justification for the rapid postwar rearming of America.[4] This document, approved by President Truman also illustrated the aggressive nature of the containment strategy:

> As to the policy of 'containment,' it is one which seeks by all means short of war to... foster the seeds of destruction within the Soviet system...[5]

Containment utilized the full resources of the burgeoning national security state. The CIA actively meddled in postwar elections to keep out Communist governments in Italy, France and Japan. In addition, it aided a number of anti-communist partisan activities in Eastern Europe as well. Such covert operations supported the general aims of President Eisenhower's 1955 directive NSC-5412/2, to:

> Create and exploit troublesome problems for International Communism, impair relations between the U.S.S.R. and Communist China and between them and their satellites.... In areas dominated

or threatened by International Communism, develop underground resistance and facilitate covert and guerrilla operations....[6]

However, where activities threatened to provoke a nuclear showdown with the Soviet Union, as in Hungary, the Eisenhower administration worked to defuse the situation, over the vociferous objections of the vehemently anti-communist forces of the American Right.

Right-wing Global Rollback

This Right espoused a more militant *global rollback* posture against "godless international communism." The major sustenance for this position came from "right-wing" business that traditionally had comprised nationally-based industries and smaller businesses with less interest in international trade than the multinationals, and which had been generally isolationist prior to World War II. In the postwar period, this grouping grew in domestic power with the American expansion to the South and West, based on the growing economic and political clout of military contractors, agribusiness and nationally-based oil companies.[7]

The major distinction between traditional conservatives and the right wing was over **how** to respond to the reality of Soviet power. Containment, originally preoccupied with the resurrection of Western Europe though the Marshall Plan and NATO, allowed the coexistence in Europe of capitalist and "socialist" systems within the acknowledged Soviet sphere of influence. Implicit was a long-term strategy of destabilizing socialist countries through propaganda efforts such as Radio Free Europe, and by ultimately ensnaring them into the logic of the world capitalist economy — in effect *long-term rollback*.

The imperial objectives of the containment advocates dovetailed with those of the global rollback forces in the *selective rollback* of many radical nationalist or socialist regimes that were considered inimical to United States corporate interests. Bipartisan efforts of the traditional conservatives and the Right resulted in ten successful rollback operations between 1950 and 1980: Korea, Iran, Guatemala, Congo, Brazil, Dominican Republic, Indonesia, Greece, Chile, and Jamaica. To carry out these objectives, the CIA was active in covert and overt operations, always providing "plausible deniability" to the Executive branch.

For these activities, U.S. intelligence agencies employed a global rollback network that spanned the military-industrial complex and foreign governments. Utilized were individuals and organizations involved in organized crime, arms trafficking, drug-running, and money-laundering, including Nazis and death squads, as well as counter-revolutionaries displaced from social revolutions in such places as China, Cuba and Nicaragua.[8]

These same networks were the agents of, in the short-term, unsuccessful rollback efforts in China, Cuba and Southeast Asia. Individuals and organizations ranging from the China Lobby through the World Anti-Communist League cooperated with U.S. intelligence and military agencies in major destabilization efforts against China that persisted up until the Nixon visit of 1972. On a number of occasions, bitter disputes erupted over whether to risk initiating a nuclear attack on China, as advocated by the Joint Chiefs of Staff during the Korean War, and later during the Quemoy and Matsu crisis. However, elite concerns about the possibility of nuclear war with the Soviet Union led to restraints being placed on the rollbackers in both situations.[9] Similarly, direct rollback activities against Cuba were ultimately phased out in the 1960s because of the Soviet nuclear umbrella that was so vividly displayed during the Cuban Missile Crisis.

Fragmentation and Reformulation of the Elite Consensus

The war in Vietnam was overwhelmingly supported by the traditional conservatives during its early years, with the aim of the selective rollback of the Hanoi government being considered fundamental to the overall containment objectives of blocking the expansion of international communism. Ultimately, the economic and political costs of the war in Vietnam led to a crisis in the postwar foreign policy consensus, culminating in the end of the Johnson Presidency.

The successor Nixon administration was a mix of influence by traditional conservative multinational business and right-wing business interests such as textiles, steel and independent oil. Foreign policy, dominated by Henry Kissinger, remained the province of the Eastern Establishment. The continued dollar drain panicked both business groups, and opposition to the war in Vietnam continued to grow among many corporate leaders. With the onset of the severe 1973-75 recession, the long period of post-WW II growth drew to a close, marking a major change for the U.S. role in the world economy.[10] The corporate elite became concerned about plummeting profitability, illustrated by the fact that the rate of after-tax profit for U.S. corporations in the 1970s was 25% below the rate in the 1960s.[11]

For one preeminent business grouping led by Chase Manhattan Bank Chairman David Rockefeller, the economic crisis required the opening of large new international markets, specifically in the socialist world of China and the Soviet Union. This proposal brought about the Kissinger-Nixon policies of détente with the Soviets and rapprochement with China.[12] In 1973, Rockefeller brought this grouping together into the Trilateral Commission. Georgia Governor Jimmy Carter was invited to join, and the Trilateral Commission successfully promoted Carter's presidential candidacy in 1976, ultimately filling 25 high level positions in Carter's administration.

Liberal Trilateralists in the State Department and the United Nations aimed to preserve the overall military balance with the U.S.S.R. through the ratification of SALT II-type arms agreements, to support peaceful conflict resolution in the Third World, and to keep the United States-Atlantic-Japanese alliance strong as the best defense against the Soviets.[13] These positions were progressively challenged by more right-leaning Trilateralists such as National Security Adviser Zbigniew Brzezinski. This wing advocated a more interventionist foreign policy to protect the interests of U.S.-based transnationals whose profits were increasingly dependent on foreign investments that were threatened by a wave of 14 Third World revolutions that took place between 1974 and 1980.[14]

By claiming that these revolutions were controlled by Moscow, policymakers also attempted to counter the effects of the *Vietnam Syndrome* — the resistance of the U.S. population to support military interventions abroad based on the collective disillusionment with the war in Indochina.

The Rise of the Committee on the Present Danger

The right-leaning Trilateralists coalesced with figures of the rising "New Right," which gained major influence within the Republican Party in the late 1970s. Right-wing publishing companies, think-tanks, religious groups, and anti-détente crusaders received millions of dollars from both right-wing oriented businesses (for example independent oil companies, protectionist textile producers represented by Jesse Helms, and raw materials producers) and from rightward moving multinationals.[15]

Right-wing business joined with right-leaning multinationals in the Committee on the Present Danger (CPD). A cross-section of businessmen and onetime military figures, the CPD strongly attacked liberal Trilateral positions favouring détente with the U.S.S.R. Making a major contribution to the ideological impact of this militarist movement were the neoconservatives who were the heirs of the pro-Vietnam War, Henry "Scoop" Jackson wing of the Democratic Party. Prominent members such as Jeanne Kirkpatrick and Irving Kristol labored mightily to promote the CPD agenda, and would later figure prominently in providing the intellectual and moral argument for the Reagan Doctrine of rolling back communism.

The CPD's efforts combined with lobbying activities by old Cold War groups such as the American Security Council in exploiting fears of a nuclear "window of vulnerability" to push the Carter administration to boost military expenditures. The overall efforts provided enormous pressure for greater hawkishness among multinationally-oriented organizations such as the Council on Foreign Relations and the U.S. Atlantic Council.[16] Military predominance would be the only guarantee of America maintaining global hegemony; as in the past, nuclear supremacy would be the ultimate insurance of the United States maintaining "escalation dominance" in any confrontation with the Soviets or their surrogates. As Paul Nitze wrote in 1979:

> To have the advantage at the utmost level of violence helps at every lesser level. In the Korean War, the Berlin blockades, and the Cuban missile crisis the United States had the ultimate edge because of our superiority at the strategic nuclear level.[17]

The militarist shift of the elites, encouraged by the events in Iran and Afghanistan, was accompanied by a reversal of the New Deal political economy, setting the stage for what would later become Reagan's domestic policies of corporate tax cuts, reduced wages and social spending, and military budget hikes to stimulate the economy. The Republican Party, with far less of a constituency for social programs and labor benefits than the Democrats, was the obvious institution for implementing the domestic program of austerity, and in 1980 virtually the entire business community threw its funds to the Reagan candidacy.[18]

The Reagan Doctrine and Global Rollback

The Reagan administration immediately set about the task of implementing the global rollback strategies that were advocated by organizations such as the Heritage Foundation, which was formed by right-wing businessman Joseph Coors and New Right strategist Paul Weyrich in 1973. It supplied detailed policy directions to the Reagan administration through its *Mandate for Leadership* volumes compiled for both terms.[19]

According to *Mandate for Leadership II*, "The president and other high administration officials have emphasized that the United States does not accept the current expanse of the Soviet empire as a permanent and irreversible feature of the historic landscape."[20]

As Heritage Foundation President Edwin Feulner, Jr., would later note in 1991:

> Heritage took the lead among think-tanks in enunciating and popularizing the Reagan Doctrine of supporting anti-Communist freedom fighters in Nicaragua, Afghanistan, Angola, Ethiopia, and elsewhere. This policy told the Soviets that they could no longer get away with the Brezhnev Doctrine, which said in effect, 'What's ours is ours, what's yours is negotiable.' The Reagan Doctrine aimed instead at expanding the free world, not simply protecting it from Communist assault, and its success forced the Soviets to come up with some "new thinking" in foreign policy.[21]

Two months after Reagan's inauguration, CIA Director William Casey presented proposals for covert actions against Nicaragua, Afghanistan, Laos, Cambodia, Grenada, Iran, Libya, and Cuba.[22] To carry out this mission, the CIA's budget was more than doubled between 1981 and 1984, and 800 of the 2,800 CIA officers who had been cashiered from the agency between 1977 and 1981 were hired back on short-term contracts.[23] On March 9, 1981, six weeks after taking office, Reagan signed a covert action plan calling for the creation of a 500-commando force and the expenditure of $19 million to conduct paramilitary operations against Nicaragua,[24] accelerating the war that would ultimately claim at least 30,000 lives.[25] Ultimately, the number of covert actions jumped from a dozen small ones in 1980, to about 40 major operations in 1986.[26]

To avoid legislative oversight that had been established in the wake of Congressional hearings on CIA activities during the late 1970s, an organization was established whose actions could be plausibly denied not only by the President but by the CIA as well. To staff this apparat, right wing ideologues inside government — led by CIA Director William Casey and National Security Council staff member Oliver North — came together with their rollback-oriented companions "outside" government, such as "retired" General Richard Secord and his coterie.

The Reagan Doctrine policy of fomenting Third World insurgencies to destabilize the Soviet Union was well articulated by neoconservative publisher Irving Kristol in a Wall Street Journal article titled "Coping with an 'Evil Empire'." Kristol aimed at provoking a split within Soviet ruling circles:

> The thrust of American foreign policy, therefore should be to inflict a series of defeats, however minor, on the Soviets. This is the significance of our support, or lack thereof, of liberation movements in Angola, Nicaragua, Afghanistan, and wherever else they emerge. The success of all such rebellions would bring into question the basic assumption of all Leninist parties as to their 'historic mission,' and their inevitable victory. Only in this way can the possibility of 'liberalization' become a reality.[27]

The Reagan Doctrine was just one component of a resurrected doctrine of "low intensity conflict" (LIC) that was not strictly military, but which included such elements as economic destabilization, political interference, and psychological operations.[28]

LIC had been a major component of the counterinsurgency strategies encouraged during the Kennedy administration for use in Latin America and Southeast Asia, utilizing Special Operations Forces (SOF) such as the

Green Berets. However, after the Vietnam War, SOF funding fell from its peak of over $1 billion per year to less than $100 million in FY 1975. As recommended by the Heritage Foundation, the Reagan administration initiated an unprecedented peacetime expansion of SOF. According to Defense Secretary Caspar Weinberger,

> The high priority we have assigned to SOF revitalization reflects our high recognition that low-level conflict — for which the SOF are uniquely suited — will pose the threat we are most likely to encounter throughout the end of the century.[29]

From 1981 through 1985, money for SOF more than tripled, with total FY 1986 funds for special operations being about $1.5 billion. Plans called for spending $7.6 billion in the five years beginning in 1988,[30] as well as having total SOF force personnel of 38,400 by 1990, representing an 80% increase over 1981.[31]

A secret five-year defense guidance plan from Secretary of Defense Weinberger ordered Special Forces to be ready "to exploit political, economic and military weaknesses within the Soviet bloc" and that "other opportunities for counter-offensives against the Soviet interests, forces, and proxy forces world-wide will be exploited to the extent possible."[32]

Pumping Up the Pentagon: Nuclear Nightmares

> The election of Ronald Reagan and the conservative tide that swept Republicans into control of the Senate in 1980 permitted the defense buildup that eventually convinced the leaders in Moscow that they couldn't keep up, especially if Reagan were as successful with SDI as he was with other defense programs. The Reagan Doctrine was vital in forcing Moscow, at last, to pay for its aggression. It also put the Soviets on the defensive. (Heritage Foundation President Edwin J. Feulner Jr.)[33]

While the Reagan Doctrine and LIC aimed at unravelling the Soviet "Empire" from the periphery, it was backed up by a massive multi-trillion dollar buildup of conventional and nuclear forces that filled the coffers of the military-industrial complex. According to a 1984 study, military contracts yielded a 25% return on equity, double the profit for manufacturing corporations in general.[34]

Reagan's militarization was fuelled by Congressional campaign donations through Political Action Committees (PACs); PAC contributions from military contractors more than tripled between 1980 and 1986.[35] The Reagan buildup was initially supported by business leadership because of its short-term stimulation of the economy. It was a key factor in the 1983-84 economic recovery; for example in March 1984, U.S. factory orders rose by the largest amount in six months; 99% of that gain was from military orders.[36]

The military buildup was aimed at the very heart of the Soviet political establishment, with the interrelated concepts of nuclear superiority, winnable nuclear war, and nuclear war-fighting becoming the dominant nuclear doctrine in the early Reagan administration. One of the first indications of this new official attitude came with National Security Decision Document 13, signed by President Reagan in 1982, proclaiming that the goal of U.S. policy is to prevail (win) in a protracted nuclear war.[37]

Central to the drive for nuclear supremacy was the Strategic Defense Initiative (SDI), or "Star Wars." The plans for SDI were hatched in 1981, at the Heritage Foundation, by a group of scientists, industrialists, military men and aerospace executives. Planners included Joseph Coors, longtime Reagan confidante Justin Dart, General Daniel Graham (affiliated with the World Anti-Communist League as well as SDI-booster organization High Frontier), and the Hoover Institution's Karl Bendetsen. Major impetus also came from Edward Teller, who is also associated with Hoover, while being associate director emeritus of the Lawrence Livermore Laboratory.

Although SDI was promoted as a "Peace Shield," its ultimate offensive nature was revealed in a statement in the Fiscal 1984-88 Defense Guidance that the Pentagon must be prepared to "wage war effectively from outer space...[and] to project force in and from outer space as needed...." In 1985, the Defense Department was reported to have devised a nuclear war plan and command structure that would integrate offensive missiles with the projected anti-missile shield embodied in the SDI,[38] that if brought to fruition, would have provided a devastating "first-strike" threat to the U.S.S.R.

However, despite the elaborate claims made for SDI by its proponents, many scientists well-acquainted with the program criticized the program as being an extreme waste of money, with computer software limitations alone making the attainment of the goal of shooting down thousands of Soviet ICBMs extremely dubious. Teller himself reportedly gave misleading and technically inaccurate reports on a key SDI weapon in secret letters to Reagan administration officials, charges corroborated by a half dozen eminent scientists long involved with the weapons lab.[39]

With the benefit of hindsight, it now appears clear that the overall thrust of the Reagan militarization program never depended on the perfect functioning of the proposed weapons systems. The threat itself was enough to exert enormous pressures on the Soviet Union, by leading it into a devastating arms race that it could afford far less than the U.S. CIA reports in 1979 documented the decline of the Soviet economy, and a 1985 CIA assessment noted that the Soviet system could not simultaneously maintain growth in defense spending, satisfy consumer demand, invest in economic modernization and support client-state economies.[40]

Accordingly, as "defense intellectual" Edward Luttwak stated in a Heritage Foundation symposium: "The real payoff of an American SDI would be its stimulation of Soviet spending on similar defenses, thereby soaking up rubles that would otherwise go for more dangerous purposes..."[41]

Elite Reappraisal of Reaganism

Massive public outcry in Europe and the United States over Reagan's "winnable nuclear war" strategies, coupled with the economic realities of the massive deficits incurred by the military outlays, caused a number of prominent multinational business leaders to criticize the Reagan defense program at the time of his 1984 reelection campaign. In May 1984 an open letter to Reagan appeared in the *New York Times* warning him that the federal deficit must be controlled, in part by reducing military spending increases. It was signed by five former Treasury Secretaries, both Democrat and Republican, and many corporate executives, with the notable absence of military contractors.[42]

With the ascension of Gorbachev to power in the U.S.S.R., arms control again returned to the forefront of U.S. foreign policy, with the State

Department pushing for the resumption of negotiations over the protests of right-wing ideologues in the administration. In addition, the steep rise in the military budget began to level off, although still in the general range of $300 billion per year. However, attacks on the periphery of the "Evil Empire" (ie., Nicaragua, Angola, etc.) continued unabated, and any dynamic moves by Gorbachev to defuse the nuclear stalemate, such as his 1985-86 unilaterally initiated 19-month moratorium on nuclear weapons testing were ignored.

However, two episodes in Reagan's second administration stand out as provoking major elite disaffection with his regime, breaking the consensus that had governed since 1981 — Reagan's conduct at the 1986 Reykjavik summit with Gorbachev, and the Contragate scandal that broke open soon afterwards.

In the case of Reykjavik, there could be no clearer indication to the traditional conservatives of the dangers posed by Reagan's personal ineptitude than his apparently sincere belief in the Right's propaganda that Star Wars was the solution to the threat of nuclear war — with Reagan stating at the summit that he was in favour of the abolition of all nuclear weapons. Reagan's call to scuttle the ultimate symbolic and terrifyingly real foundation of Western power antagonized the transnational (NATO) corporate aristocracy, leading to the unprecedented "correction" of the President by Secretary of State George Schultz in the immediate post-summit period.

Iran-Contragate led to further disaffection of the elites, as expressed by veteran conservative foreign policy expert Robert W. Tucker, who observed that "As a textbook example in how not to conduct foreign policy, it will be hard to improve upon. (Reykjavik almost did so though. Coming at the same time that the Iranian scandal broke, it has prompted more than one otherwise sympathetic observer to wonder whether the administration is still able to conduct a coherent and effective foreign policy.)" Criticizing the Iran initiative for its "breathtaking incompetence," Tucker was clear in his disdain for those administration figures who conducted foreign policy without traditional counsel: "Had more been known...by those who were entitled to know and should have known,...it seems safe to say that disaster would not have occurred."[43]

While Ronald Reagan and his right-wing allies drew criticism from Congress and the entire nation, the scope of the investigation remained extremely limited, with the leadership of the House and Senate committees specifically avoiding delving into the history of the CIA-linked proprietaries and global rollback networks. Thus, while Ollie North and his colleagues were temporarily scapegoated, the CIA's capabilities for covert and illegal interventionist operations remained protected for the future.

The Contragate investigation never challenged the policy of rolling-back the Sandinista government; while the hearings were in progress Congress failed to cut off $40 million for the contras, which it had the power to do. In addition, the administration was permitted to provide $15 million in new military assistance to the insurgent forces in Angola.[44]

However, from Contragate onward, the aggressive rollback policies of the Right were held in check. Although *Policy Review* Assistant Editor Michael Johns asserted that "...Seven years after Ronald Reagan's arrival in Washington, the United States government and its allies are still dominated by the culture of appeasement that drove Neville Chamberlain to Munich in 1938...,"[45] Mikhael Gorbachev and his "useful idiot" Ronald Reagan reached an accord in 1987 to eliminate intermediate range nuclear forces in Europe.[46]

As the Reagan administration drew to a close, the obvious changes in the U.S.S.R. and Eastern Europe facilitated by Gorbachev even led to "new thinking" being expressed in the Heritage Foundation's *Policy Review*. In the lead article in the Winter 1988 issue, a unique strategy was proposed for moving the Gorbachev-type reformers towards the formation of a non-socialist, Russian-nationalist authoritarian state that could be a potential future ally. To facilitate this, the author proposed a "Grand Bargain" that would involve the United States and its allies providing large-scale economic and technical assistance to the U.S.S.R. — a "Marshall Plan for Post-Soviet Russia."[47]

Preparing for the "New World Order": Discriminate Deterrence

With the Cold War winding down, the time was ripe for elite reassessment of U.S. foreign policy priorities. The Commission on Integrated Long-Term Strategy on January 10, 1988 issued its *Discriminate Deterrence* report that would set the basic approach of the United States in confronting global challenges until the end of the century.

The Commission included such notables as Henry Kissinger and Zbigniew Brzezinski, and called for continued military pressure to be placed on the U.S.S.R. However, *Discriminate Deterrence* represented a major change in strategic focus, advocating a shift in military resources from Europe to the Third World through a buildup of high-tech conventional weaponry and an increased capacity to wage conventional and "low intensity" warfare. The report also championed the production of new powerful non-nuclear as well as nuclear munitions that could be developed and delivered with pin-point accuracy through space-age technologies of the sort embraced by the SDI. The recommendations provided a framework for the priorities of the following Bush administration, heralding the later developments of the 1991 Gulf War.[48]

George Bush was the perfect candidate to lead the country into what would become the "post-Soviet" era. A product of Eastern elite upbringing who was well-connected to the Sunbelt bankrollers of right-wing Republicanism, he represented a coalition that would press the pursuit of Reagan's domestic agenda of slashed social spending, while relying on military power to protect U.S. interests. However, as denoted by his cabinet choices, the Bush administration would return the conduct of foreign policy to the traditional leadership that strove to finally integrate the world, including the rapidly collapsing Soviet bloc, into the matrix of capitalist relationships. The military option would be reserved for those who did not have the sense to know their place in the unfolding new world order.

In terms of the Third World, the administration was able to harvest the fruits of the previous decade's "low intensity" assault on liberation movements and socialist/radical nationalist governments. The intensity of the contra war was lessened somewhat, with the Bush administration agreeing to pursue the electoral process in Nicaragua, over the strenuous objections of the Right. The resulting defeat of the Sandinistas at the polls was testimony to the potency of the combined strategy of contra war carried out by the rollback networks, and the long-term policy of diplomatic isolation and economic destabilization that emanated from the State Department. Similarly, the economic and military pressures on Angola, Cambodia/Vietnam, and Ethiopia carried out under the aegis of supporting "freedom fighters" led to "victories" for the United States as well.

However, the uncelebrated part of the harvest was the unprecedented level of global emiseration and instability that flowed from the austerity policies carried out by organizations such as the International Monetary Fund (IMF). By the mid-1980s, Third World debt was approximately $800 billion, much of it concentrated in Latin America.[49] While the Reagan administration had spent billions of dollars to overthrow the Sandinistas and support the death squad regime in El Salvador, Latin America experienced its "lost decade," with average incomes in 1988 having fallen to the level of 1978. During this same period, an estimated $170 billion in flight capital left Latin America; with total anonymous capital flows, including drug money and flight capital being estimated as high as $600 billion to $800 billion.[50]

While the grievous Third World conditions were attributed to failures to fully employ strategies of "privatization," the Bush administration readied its military and intelligence agencies for another decade of "low intensity conflict."

Things were set in motion soon after Bush's inauguration. In early 1989, reversing perhaps the only positive outcome of the Contragate hearings, Speaker of the House Jim Wright shelved a bill that would have restricted CIA covert activities by requiring timely notification of Congress.[51] At about the same time, CIA Director Webster, warning of unrest and "coup-plotting" in Latin America, called for a bipartisan policy to support covert actions in the Western hemisphere, including backing the region's military as a force for stability.[52]

A major device to facilitate U.S. military intervention and support of counterinsurgency in the region had already been instituted in 1986 when President Reagan issued a national security directive officially declaring drugs a "national security threat" and authorizing U.S. military involvement in a wide range of anti-narcotics activities. The Omnibus Antidrug Abuse Act of 1988 called for a substantial increase in military aid to countries involved in U.S. antinarcotics programs; at the time this included $3.5 million in military aid for the antinarcotics units of the South American police forces, waiving a 1974 ban on aid to foreign police. Exceptions to the same ban allowed the U.S. military to train Bolivian and Columbian police forces in antinarcotics activities as well.[53]

A number of counterinsurgency enthusiasts saw "low intensity conflict" against the drug traffickers as representing a legitimate role for the armed forces. Army Colonel John Waghelstein, former commander of the U.S. military advisers in El Salvador, called for strong Pentagon action "to counter the guerrilla/narcotics terrorists in this hemisphere." Such action, he stated, would provide the Pentagon with an "unassailable moral position" from which to counter the "church and academic groups" that have resisted U.S. intervention in Central America.[54]

In September 1989, Defense Secretary Cheney remarked that drugs were "a direct threat to the sovereignty and security of our country." According to Bush administration officials, Pentagon leaders believed that getting involved in the "War on Drugs" could help the military preserve its power as East-West tensions were declining. "With peace breaking out all over," one two-star general said in an interview, "it might give us something to do."[55] The stage was set for the invasion of Panama, with all the attendant media glorification and photo opportunities.

However, the "success" of the relatively limited operation in Panama was no test of the difficulties that the military would face in a protracted drug war/counterinsurgency against present and future guerrilla movements. Previous "invited" U.S. military incursions, such as the 1986 *Operation Blast Furnace* in Bolivia and the 1988 *Operation Snowcap* spanning the coca-growing regions of both Bolivia and Peru caused, at most, small and temporary declines in cocaine supply. In addition, the Peruvian operations tended to drive peasants into supporting the Sendero Luminoso revolutionaries, causing Operation Snowcap to be cancelled because the safety of U.S. military personnel could not be guaranteed.[56]

Although President Bush in 1990 pledged $423 million for anti-drug efforts in the Andean countries, U.S. anti-drug efforts have to date failed to deal with the fact that the cocaine trade has been almost the only industry keeping the devastated Andean economies alive. Coca is Peru's most important export, generating between $800 million to $1.2 billion in foreign exchange, representing at least 30% of the total value of all other exports combined.[57] The approximately $90 million that the United States pledged to Peru in early 1991 for military efforts against the drug trade will likely lead to additional human rights violations, but cannot make a dent in the underlying economic crisis that fuels the industry.[58] With no public mandate for heavier intervention on behalf of muddled aims, U.S. military involvement currently remains on a holding pattern.

Kicking the Vietman Syndrome: Bush's Gulf War

With the collapse of the Eastern bloc commencing in the fall of 1989, the image of the "Evil Empire" that had justified the bloated military budgets of the 1980s ceased to persuade the American people that they should forestall dealing with the deteriorating conditions of U.S. society. With the rising demand for a "Peace Dividend," the Gulf War occurred at just the right time for American militarists. Again, citing Heritage Foundation President Edwin Feulner Jr.:

> The President's leadership in the Gulf War was also tremendously important for conservatives. The war proved to the American people that the taxpayer funds we've been spending on defense were worth it. It proved to the military and the civilian leaders in the Department of Defense that it's sometimes appropriate to use your fancy weapons, and not just strut them around on the parade ground. Finally, and this can't be overstated, the war revealed America's primary leadership role in the world.[59]

While the slogan "No Blood for Oil" was criticized by media pundits and war-boosters as being too simplistic, it did capture the essence of the economic and political relationships that fuelled the war. Of primary concern to President Bush and his fellow-warriors was maintaining secure political control over Mideast petroleum through maintaining the alliances with regimes such as Saudi Arabia that guaranteed relatively stable oil supplies and "moderate" prices. Just as important was conserving the systems that facilitated the circulation of petrodollars that were invested in Western banks, such as the over $100 billion from Kuwait,[60] and which purchased modern weaponry. These relationships were extremely profitable to the military-industrial complexes of the entire NATO alliance, as well as of the Soviet Union.

According to a report prepared by the Congressional Research Service, the five permanent members of the U.N. Security Council supplied more than $163.2 billion worth of weapons and military equipment to Mideast nations during a 14-year period before imposing an arms embargo on Iraq. Mideast nations bought almost $214 billion worth of advanced weapons and medium level technology between 1974 and 1988, with more than 75% coming from the Security Council members. The leading arms merchant was the Soviet Union ($74 billion), followed by the United States at $44 billion.[61]

Despite the threat posed to the matrix of oil/petrodollar/arms relationships by the Iraqi invasion of Kuwait, U.S. elite and military opinion was very divided over the choice of waiting for economic sanctions to work versus going to war. Divisions even spread to some portions of the Right, with Patrick Buchanan demurring from supporting the war because of fears of the United States getting caught in a quagmire.[62] With over 60,000 body-bags being sent to the Gulf in anticipation of armed conflict, leaders such as former Joint Chiefs of Staff William Crowe were concerned about the effects of massive American casualties on public opinion that had not been fully weaned from the "Vietnam Syndrome" by the previous decade's demonstration wars in Grenada, Libya, and Panama.

However, President Bush prevailed in drumming up the necessary elite and Congressional backing for the war, utilizing an effective public-relations campaign that employed organizations well-connected to the Right, such as the Coalition for America at Risk.[63] In so doing, Bush effectively played on the fears of alleged Iraqi capabilities in chemical, biological and nuclear weaponry. Conveniently ignored was the fact that $500 million worth of advanced American manufactured goods were sold to Iraq from 1985 until up to a day before the August 1990 invasion of Kuwait, including sales to Iraqi offices that have been publicly identified as research centres for ballistic missiles or nuclear and chemical weapons.[64]

More important, it was not reported that the United States had been the main obstacle to curbing the Third World proliferation of nuclear weapons, demonstrated by its wrecking a tentative accord reached in the summer of 1990 by the parties to the Nuclear Non-Proliferation Treaty (NPT). This draft accord, which would have tightened export controls on weapons-grade materials and strengthened inspection procedures for potential weapons sites, foundered on the refusal of the United States to end the testing of nuclear weapons.[65]

Of central concern to the Gulf warriors was asserting the preeminent U.S. role as sole superpower and gendarme for the post- Cold War new world order. As such, the policy was aimed as much at reigning supreme over European and Japanese allies who, being much more dependent on Mideast oil, would necessarily defer to U.S. military dominance in the region.

With careful media and "perception" management that characterized the ensuing video-arcade war, the high-tech wonder of the U.S. arsenal was trumpeted for its efficiency and "kinder, gentler" methods of slaughter. The military-industrial complex was ecstatic at the promotion of Stealth systems, "smart" weaponry and Patriot missiles, with original reports greatly exaggerating their effectiveness. It wasn't until the Fall of 1991 that it was revealed that the Patriot missiles destroyed no more than 20 percent of Scud missile warheads,[66] and that the use of the Patriots may have increased the amount of explosive debris over Israel and Saudi Arabia.[67]

Nevertheless, the aftermath of the war provided a potential bonanza for the arms merchants. The administration immediately proposed to sell some $33 billion in new weapons in 1991, two-thirds in the Mideast, much to Israel and Saudi Arabia. Included is a Saudi purchase of over 700 Patriot missiles for $3.3 billion, and a sale of $1.6 billion worth of new weapons to Egypt[68], facilitated by Bush's 1990 forgiving of a $7 billion arms debt for Egypt's cooperation in the Gulf War.[69]

In addition to continuing to fuel an arms race in the Mideast that could lead to a future conflagration, Bush's recent policies regarding nuclear, chemical and biological weapons (CBW) negated his pre-war propaganda calling for strong international accords to curb their proliferation. Bush reversed his previous call for fully open and immediate inspections regarding chemical weapons, because of concerns that such inspections of U.S. sites would expose top-secret information regarding new Stealth technologies, etc.[70] In addition, Bush rejected Congressional attempts to tighten export controls on materials integral to the production of chemical, biological, and nuclear weapons, claiming that such legislation would hamper the Executive's prerogatives on foreign policy.[71]

However, despite Bush's immediate post-war boast of having finally "kicked the Vietnam Syndrome once and for all,"[72] it was far from clear that the American public, who had been shielded from a protracted war with massive U.S. casualties, could be counted on to support interventions in the future. In addition, the obvious post-war chaos, including the situation of the Kurds and the well-publicized intra-administration recriminations over the failure to eliminate Saddam Hussein, tarnished the victory, miles of yellow ribbons notwithstanding.

The Final Collapse of the Evil Empire

In the meantime, the Right continued its heavy involvement rolling-back any vestiges of socialism in the newly "liberated" countries of Eastern Europe. Leaders of the Right affiliated with organizations such as the American Enterprise Institute and the Heritage Foundation played key roles in advising new conservative leaders on how to denationalize state enterprises and promote free market economies. For the obvious social dislocations that would accompany the resultant high inflation and massive unemployment, particularly among women, right-wing evangelical organizations ranging from the Moonies to fundamentalist Christians aimed to promote an agenda based on "traditional values," including the reversal of abortion rights.[73]

New Right founder Paul Weyrich and his Free Congress Foundation (FCF) have been particularly active in Eastern Europe. In the Soviet Union, FCF sponsored numerous training sessions for Boris Yeltsin's organization, with FCF claiming that it "trained the Yeltsin group in its effort to win control of the Russian Republic."[74] In addition, Yeltsin reportedly used FCF instructions in media manipulation to help smash the hardliner's coup.[75] Since the coup, televangelist Pat Robertson's organization has been actively proselytizing in the U.S.S.R., aiming to get 20 million Christian converts by the end of 1991. To facilitate this, Robertson's group broadcasts regularly on Russian television, due to strong relations developed with high-ranking individuals from Russian State television.[76]

Although the collapse of the Soviet Union provided the Right with unprecedented opportunities to promote its social agenda, it also removed the primary rationale for continuing to support massive expenditures for conventional and nuclear weapons in the European theatre. In July 1991, Bush and Gorbachev signed the START Treaty that cut the number of nuclear warheads by about 30%. In September, Bush unilaterally withdrew all land and sea tactical nuclear weapons for disposal or storage, and in October Gorbachev unilaterally ordered a 17%

greater cut in the number of Soviet ICBMs than was required by START, while implementing a unilateral one-year ban on nuclear tests. The United States remained steadfast in its refusal to stop testing weapons, because of its desire to modernize its arsenal.[77]

These cuts were celebrated by the world community, with pressure for much deeper cuts coming from a number of elite figures, including some long-associated with the weapons labs. For example, in September 1991 a committee of nuclear weapons experts at the National Academy of Sciences, including former Livermore Lab Director Michael May and ex-Chair of the Joint Chiefs of Staff General David Jones, reported that strategic warheads now held by both the United States and the U.S.S.R. could be slashed by 90% without endangering either nation's security.[78] In such a situation, the development of an SDI system by the United States would permit it to maintain strategic dominance.

The Right attacked Bush for "unilateral disarmament."[79] However, Bush's cuts spared submarine-based strategic missiles, the most invulnerable component of the U.S. nuclear arsenal, leaving the United States with unchallenged strategic superiority. In addition, because of U.S. insistence, the START Treaty does not require the actual destruction of missiles, allowing their reuse for the revitalized SDI program.[80]

Bush's push for Star Wars has been given critical support by the Right, utilizing the hype generated by the "success" of the Patriot missile. As Angelo Codevilla of the Hoover Institute recommended in 1991:

> Once a decision is made to build anti-missile defenses, the opposition from the *New York Times* editorial page, the MIT physics department, the Arms Control Association, and key members of the Democratic Party can easily be overcome. All the President would have to do is ask the American people whether they would rather be in the position of the Israelis before or after they had Patriots.[81]

Citing the danger of possible chaos in the degenerating Soviet state, as well as potential Third World nuclear threats, the administration has moved away from the discredited model of a "Peace Shield" on which $27 billion was squandered during the last decade. In late 1990, the SDI metamorphosed into the *Global Protection Against Limited Strikes (GPALS)* system, intended to defend against tactical and theatre missile threats as well as up to 200 strategic missile warheads launched against the United States. While the administration estimates a cost of $41 billion, extrapolation from similar projects suggests a probable cost of more than $150 billion.[82]

In November 1991, President Bush and the Right scored a major political victory in getting Congress to agree to allocate $4.2 billion for SDI in the FY 1992 budget.[83] The continuation of SDI is a key component in the U.S. attempt to maintain military supremacy in Bush's new world order. Once even a limited space-based SDI system is in place, it would theoretically expand U.S. military capabilities beyond the sophistication displayed in the Gulf War, when Baghdad's early-warning systems were knocked out, leaving it vulnerable to even the "dumbest" of missiles. By giving the United States the ultimate "high ground," SDI would provide the military with the ability to counter the effects of dispersal of high-tech systems such as Stealth to the Third World.[84] Or, in the words of Reagan's Undersecretary of the Air Force Edward Aldridge: "We do not have to stretch our imagination very far to see that the nation that controls space may control the world."[85]

Beyond Rollback

At this juncture, global rollback in its classic conception seems to have been virtually accomplished, although the Right continues to push the Bush administration to pursue more aggressive actions against Cuba, Vietnam and China, including a call for establishing a "Radio-Free Asia."[86]

However, as the recent battles over the military budget indicate, there is likely to be continued debate between those advocating different conceptions of America's future. On the one hand, the present project of the Right, apparently supported by the Bush administration, is for continued prioritizing of military power as the ultimate guarantor of "national security." Some observers, such as Michael Vlahos, the director of the State Department's Center for the Study of Foreign Affairs, have called for pursuing dominance in the high-tech military realm, as with SDI, to bolster the U.S. competitive position versus the Japanese and Europeans.[87]

On the other hand, many members of the traditional elite, themselves flush with the satisfaction of having negated the "world socialist system," have been raising fundamental questions about the wisdom of continuing to waste a substantial portion of the nation's present and future resources on weapons.

With a budget deficit for 1991 of approximately $300 billion,[88] a Savings and Loan bailout cost presently estimated at $500 billion, and inestimable costs of stably integrating the former "Evil Empire" into the capitalist system, it is difficult to imagine how an elite consensus can be maintained on spending $300 billion a year on the military.

The Peace Dividend has become an issue for the traditional conservatives, not due to any primary desire to provide decent human services to the population, but because there is general concern that the continued deterioration of society (ie., infrastructure, education) will result in the United States falling significantly behind the Japanese and Europeans. U.S. military power has certainly provided the United States with significant clout vis-à-vis its *present* allies, as witness the Gulf War and the continued acceptance by Europe of U.S. leadership in NATO. However, there are increasing signs that Europe wants to wean itself from paying too much "protection" to the United States, as NATO conceptions are reformed while Europe moves towards economic integration.[89]

The elites realize that although military power was essential for rolling back the U.S.S.R., at a minimum by accelerating internal Soviet pressures, it has come at an enormous cost of capital. From 1949 to 1989, the total budget of the Department of Defense (in 1982 dollars) was $8.2 trillion. This was greater than the monetary value of civilian industry's plant and equipment and of the nation's infrastructure in 1982, a total of $7.3 trillion. In every year from 1951 to 1990, the Pentagon budget has exceeded the combined net profits of all American corporations.[90]

Thus, the costs of restoring U.S. competitiveness will likely lead to growing pressure from the elites to pare the military budget of expensive items that, with the Soviet collapse, have no real strategic value, such as the Stealth bomber. In addition, consensus is rapidly growing to make significant cuts in the strategic nuclear arsenal, perhaps as much as 90 per cent.

However, as indicated in "Discriminate Deterrence," elite requirements to contain Third World explosions will consistently generate pressures to develop new, sophisticated and very expensive weapons systems, such as those that will likely emanate from the new SDI program.

Such weaponry cannot resolve the structural basis of a burgeoning world economic crisis, well summarized by Charles Cerami of the Atlantic Council of the United States:

> Unless we start now to create new jobs by the millions in scores of countries, some of the most difficult years that man has ever known may be facing us... The underlying global trend is for more and more persons to compete for a scanty supply of jobs...the jobless hordes are building to a 'critical mass' that could be harder to control than any nuclear arsenal.[91]

Cerami's description no longer applies to just the Third World, but also to the unfolding climate of economic dislocation in the former "Evil Empire." Already, hordes of "economic refugees" have fled to Western Europe, met by a rising tide of xenophobia, exemplified by recent attacks by neo-Nazis on migrant settlements.[92] In such an atmosphere, the regressive solutions offered by the Right, in the United States and abroad, may increasingly resonate within ruling circles.

The transnational elites, faced with the looming possibility of world economic collapse, will likely intensify the policies of austerity capitalism imposed by sheer force in the Third World, and progressively incorporate such policies to maintain rule at home. Thus, the most enduring and unfortunate legacy of a half century of "rollback" may well be a new world order characterized by generalized authoritarian rule and institutionalized terror.

Notes

1. "Conservative Movement Should Take Well-Deserved Bow," *Human Events*, September 7, 1991.
2. Walter Isaacson and Evan Thomas, *The Wise Men*. New York: Simon and Schuster, 1986; Laurence Shoup and William Minter, *Imperial Brain Trust*. New York: Monthly Review Press, 1977; Holly Sklar, Trilateralism. Montreal, Black Rose Books, 1980.
3. Mr. X, "The Sources of Soviet Conduct" *Foreign Affairs*, July 1947.
4. Tom Gervasi, *The Myth of Soviet Superiority*. New York: Harper and Row, 1987, p. 218.
5. Thomas Etzold and John Gaddis, *Containment: Documents on American Policy and Strategy, 1945-1950*. New York: Columbia University Press, 1978, pp. 385-442.
6. Franz Schurmann, *The Logic of World Power*. New York: Pantheon Books, 1974, p. 413.

7. Kirkpatrick Sale, *Power Shift*. New York: Vintage Books, 1976, p. 100.
8. Alfred McCoy, *The Politics of Heroin: CIA Complicity in the Global Drug Trade*. Brooklyn: Lawrence Hill Books, 1991; Christopher Simpson, *Blowback* New York: Macmillan Publishing Company, 1988; Jonathon Marshall, Peter Dale Scott, and Jane Hunter, *The Iran Contra Connection*. Montréal: Black Rose Books, 1987; Leslie Cockburn, *Out of Control*. New York: Atlantic Monthly Press, 1987; Scott Anderson and Jon Anderson, *Inside the League*. New York: Dodd Mead and Company, 1986.
9. Michio Kaku and Daniel Axelrod, *To Win a Nuclear War: The Pentagon's Secret War Plans*. Montréal: Black Rose Books, 1987, pp. 1-2, 72-73, 107.
10. Thomas Ferguson and Joel Rogers, *Right Turn*. New York: Hill and Wang, 1986, pp. 68-74.
11. New York Times, October 9, 1986.
12. Ferguson and Rogers, p. 94; Holly Sklar, *Trilateralism*. Montréal: Black Rose Books, 1980, pp. 448-50.
13. Sklar, p. 570.
14. Fred Halliday, The Making of the Second Cold War. London: Verso Editions, 1983, p. 92.
15. Ferguson and Rogers, pp. 103-105.
16. Ferguson and Rogers, pp. 98-99.
17. "Is SALT a Fair Deal?," in Charles Tyroler, *Alerting America: The Papers of the Committee on the Present Danger*. Washington D.C.: Pergamon-Brassey's International Defense Publishers, 1984, p. 160.
18. Ferguson and Rogers, p. 78.
19. Ferguson and Rogers, pp. 89-92.
20. Stuart Butler, et al., *Mandate for Leadership II*. Washington D.C.: The Heritage Foundation, 1984, p. 285
21. Edwin J. Feulner Jr., "Conservatism's Growing Pains," *Policy Review* No. 58, Fall 1991, p. 6.
22. *Miami Herald*, June 5, 1983.
23. John Prados, *Presidents' Secret Wars*. New York: William Morrow and Company, 1986, pp. 366, 369.
24. *Washington Post*, February 14, March 10 and 16, 1982 and May 8, 1983.
25. Noam Chomsky, "The Decline of the Democratic Ideal," *Z Magazine*, May 1990, p. 28.
26. *New York Times*, July 7, 1986.
27. *Wall Street Journal*, December 17, 1985.
28. John Waghelstein, "Post-Vietnam Counterinsurgency Doctrine," *Military Review*, May 1985.
29. Center for Defense Information, *The Defense Monitor*, Vol. 14, No. 2, 1985.
30. *New York Times*, July 19, 1986.
31. Center for Defense Information, *The Defense Monitor*, Vol. 14, No. 2, 1985.
32. Ronnie Dugger, *On Reagan*. New York: McGraw-Hill Book Company, 1983, p. 353.
33. Edwin J. Feulner Jr., "Conservatism's Growing Pains," *Policy Review* No. 58, Fall 1991, pp. 11-12.
34. *New York Times*, April 9, 1985.
35. *New York Times*, April 9, 1985.
36. *Fortune*, April 30, 1984; Gerald Pascall, *The Trillion Dollar Budget*. Seattle: University of Washington Press, 1985, p. 164.
37. Robert Scheer. *With Enough Shovels*. New York: Vintage Books, 1983, pp. 3, 12.
38. Michio Kaku and Daniel Axelrod, p. 15; *New York Times*, May 29, 1985.
39. Dan Stober. "Teller Exaggerated 'Star Wars', Scientists Say," *San José Mercury News*, February 4, 1988.

40. *New York Times*, November 5, 1991.
41. "The Defense Budget: A Conservative Debate," *Policy Review*, Summer 1985.
42. *New York Times*, May 4, 1984.
43. Robert Tucker, "Fouling Up," *The National Interest*, Spring 1987, pp. 93-96.
44. *New York Times*, June 11, 1987.
45. Michael Johns, "Peace in Our Time." *Policy Review*, Summer 1987, pp. 69-71.
46. *Human Events*, January 23, 1988, p. 21.
47. David Moro, "The National Rebirth of Russia. A U.S. Strategy for Lifting the Soviet Siege," *Policy Review*, Winter 1988.
48. Report of the Commission on Integrated Long-Term Strategy. "Discriminate Deterrence," Washington D.C: U.S. government Printing Office, 1988; New York Times, January 11, 1988; San Francisco Examiner, January 13, 1988.
49. André Gunder Frank, "Defuse the Debt Bomb? When Apparent Solutions Become Real Problems," *World Policy Journal*, Summer, 1984.
50. Jeff Gerth, "U.S. Seeks Tougher Line on Flight Capital," *New York Times*, February 12, 1990; Chomsky, N. "The Victors: II" *Z Magazine*, January 1991.
51. *New York Times*, February 1, 1989.
52. *San Francisco Chronicle*, February 9, 1989.
53. Peter Andreas and Coletta Younger, "U.S. Drug Policy and the Andean Cocaine Industry," *World Policy Journal*, Summer 1989.
54. Michael Klare, "A Blueprint for Endless Intervention," *The Nation*, July 30 to August 6, 1988.
55. Douglas Jehl and Melissa Healy, "Armed Forces Want to Be Drug Warriors," *San Francisco Chronicle*, December 15, 1989.
56. Michael Klare, "Fighting Drugs with the Military," *The Nation*, January 1, 1990; Peter Andreas, and Coletta Younger, "U.S. Drug Policy and the Andean Cocaine Industry," *World Policy Journal*, Summer 1989.
57. "Courage in Columbia," *New York Times* Editorial, February 15, 1990; Michael Klare, "Fighting Drugs with the Military," *The Nation*, January 1, 1990; Peter Andreas, and Coletta Younger, "U.S. Drug Policy and the Andean Cocaine Industry," *World Policy Journal*, Summer 1989.
58. "Peru Accepts U.S. Help in Battling Cocaine," *San Francisco Chronicle*, May 16, 1991.
59. Edwin J. Feulner Jr., "Conservatism's Growing Pains," *Policy Review* No. 58, Fall 1991, p. 7.
60. *The Nation*, September 10, 1990.
61. *San Francisco Chronicle*, May 6, 1991.
62. Sara Diamond, "Rumble on the Right," *Z Magazine*, December 1980.
63. Ibid.
64. Michael Wines, "U.S. Tells of Prewar Technology Sales to Iraq Worth $500 Million," *New York Times*, March 12, 1991.
65. Leonard Spector and Jacqueline Smith, "Treaty Review: Deadlock Damages Nonproliferation," *The Bulletin of the Atomic Scientists*, December 1990.
66. Eric Schmitt, "Israel Plays Down Effectiveness of Patriot Missile," *New York Times*, October 31, 1991.
67. Eric Schmitt, "Saudis to Buy 14 More Batteries of Patriot Missiles From the U.S., *New York Times*, November 9, 1991.
68. "Poison Gas: Only Part of the Problem," *New York Times* Editorial, March 12, 1991; *New York Times*, November 9, 1991.
69. Michael Klare, " Fueling the Fire: How We Armed the Middle East," *The Bulletin of the Atomic Scientists*; Vol 47, No. 1; January/February 1991, pp. 19-26.

70. Paul Lewis, "U.S. Now Prefers Limited Inspection on Chemical Arms," *New York Times*, August 14, 1991.
71. "White House Fights Bill on Nuclear Exports," *San Francisco Chronicle*, October 15, 1991.
72. Noam Chomsky, "'What We Say Goes': The Middle East in the New World Order," *Z Magazine*, May 1991, p. 52.
73. Eleanor Randolph, "Invasion of the Pious," *San Francisco Chronicle*, November 3, 1991; Russ Bellant and Louis Wolf, "The Free Congress Foundation Goes East," *Covert Action Information Bulletin*, No. 35, Fall 1990.
74. Russ Bellant and Louis Wolf, "The Free Congress Foundation Goes East," *Covert Action Information Bulletin*, No. 35, Fall 1990.
75. *Washington Times*, August 27, 1991.
76. "700 Club," Christian Broadcasting Network, September 17, 1991.
77. Keay Davidson, "Experts Dare to Imagine a Nuke-Free U.S.," *San Francisco Examiner*, November 3, 1991; Flora Lewis, "End Nuclear Tests? Yes. Now," *New York Times*, October 22, 1991.
78. David Perlman, "U.S. Weapons Experts Urge Deep Cuts in Nuclear Arms," *San Francisco Chronicle*, September 6, 1991; Carl Kaysen, Robert McNamara, and George Rathjens, "Nuclear Weapons After the Cold War," *Foreign Affairs*, Vol. 70, No.4, Fall 1991.
79. "Bush Stumbles with Unilateral Disarmament Moves," *Human Events*, October 12, 1991.
80. R. Jeffrey Smith, "U.S.–Soviet Arms Pact's Odd Feature," *San Francisco Chronicle*, August 15, 1991.
81. Angelo Codevilla, "A Question of Patriot-ism," *Policy Review* No. 56, Spring 1991.
82. John Pike and Christopher Bolkom, "Reincarnated Star Wars is Still a Turkey," *San Francisco Examiner*, May 6, 1991.
83. Eric Schmitt, "Soviet Upheaval Has Little Impact on Military Spending Compromise," *New York Times*, November 2, 1991.
84. William Perry, "Desert Storm and Deterrence," *Foreign Affairs*, Vol. 70, No.4, Fall 1991; Robert Hurwitt, "The Star Wars Encounter," *East Bay Express*, September 13, 1991.
85. Center for Defense Information, "Nuclear Warfighting Quotations by Reagan Administration Officials and Supporters," September 1983.
86. James Tyson, "Time to Create a Radio-Free Asia," *Human Events*, September 14, 1991.
87. Vlahos, M. "Culture and Foreign Policy," *Foreign Policy*, No. 82, Spring 1991.
88. Robert Pear, "'90 Pact Failing to Curb Deficit, Lawmakers Say," *New York Times*, November 4, 1991.
89. *New York Times*, November 8, 1991.
90. Seymour Melman, "Military State Capitalism," *The Nation*, May 20, 1991.
91. *New York Times*, January 13, 1985.
92. *New York Times*, November 3, 1991.

Chapter Three

The Real Stakes in the Gulf War*

Samir Amin

The Gulf War as it was presented in the Western media had but one objective: to enforce the rule of law and under that banner to liberate Kuwait. Once this objective was met, it was claimed, a "new world order" founded on law and justice would be established, finally realizing the promise of the end of the East-West conflict.

Nothing whatever gives credence to this claim. Quite to the contrary, the Gulf War will necessarily heighten the injustices that are the foundation of all world orders, new and old. It is certain that the principal Western powers will not reconstruct the world so that it is more just, but on the contrary will reaffirm an order that — in the five hundred years since the conquest of the Americas and the genocide of their native populations began — has constantly violated the rights of the peoples of Asia, Africa, and Latin America. This is an order that Mr. Bush and his European allies cannot conceivably intend to undermine.

For half a century this world order has pursued in the Middle East a single overriding objective, to perpetuate what is euphemistically called access to oil, under terms that unmistakably ensure the command of the Western powers over this resource. To attain this objective, two com-

---
* This chapter, first presented in April 1991 at the International Sociological Association meeting in Vancouver, was translated by Locke Anderson, and published in *Monthly Review*, Vol. 43, No. 3 (July-August 1991).

plementary means are to be employed: first, the perpetuation of the division of the Arab world and the assured survival of the archaic regimes of the Gulf — Saudi Arabia, Kuwait, the Emirates, and Qatar — in a manner that precludes any possibility that their wealth will be used in the service of all the Arab peoples; and second, the guarantee of the absolute military supremacy of Israel (which has been helped to arm itself with nuclear weapons) in a manner that gives it the power to intervene instantaneously whenever it decides that it is necessary to do so.

The United States had to involve its forces directly to destroy Iraq's military potential. This decision was taken by Washington and Tel Aviv around May 1990. If Tel Aviv alone had been able to do the job, it would have done so under some pretext like that used in 1956 against Egypt. But the Iran-Iraq war had induced the West to furnish Saddam Hussein with arms that made him a definite military threat to Israel. The work of the destruction of Iraq had consequently to be a direct enterprise of the Western armies. The invasion of Kuwait, which had been preceded by many provocations, served as an adequate pretext. We know almost certainly now that this invasion was a trap set by Washington into which Saddam Hussein, encouraged by the U.S. Ambassador to Baghdad, had fallen. In invading Kuwait, Saddam Hussein destroyed the equilibrium that guaranteed the regimes of the Gulf.

On August 2, 1990, therefore, no diplomat worthy of the name was genuinely surprised, although some pretended to be. At no point in the diplomatic initiative did the Western powers credibly propose to discuss among the principals of the world order the right of the Palestinians to a state of their own or the right of the Arab peoples to use their petroleum riches for their own purposes. Up until August 2 Saddam Hussein had suggested that negotiations of these issues accompany negotiations over Kuwait. The Western diplomats put up a stone wall of refusal, because they had already decided on war.

North versus South

The Gulf War was therefore a North-South conflict. The nature of the Iraqi regime and the personality of Saddam Hussein were not without importance, certainly, but they were secondary. This intervention by an unprecedented armed force will hardly generate respect for international law or re-establish democracy in Iraq. It will simply maintain the political and petroleum status quo in the Middle East.

Saddam Hussein had been supported by the West for more than a decade, including the years of his criminal and fruitless combat with Iran, because he had served the interests of the West. Never has he been a democrat. Wasn't the pretext of democracy a bit ridiculous anyhow in a war to defend Saudi Arabia and restore the emir of Kuwait?

The argument of "international law" was not much better. What has the West done to force Israel to respect UN Resolution 242 and to evacuate the territories it has illegally occupied for twenty years? When has the West challenged the illegal annexation of Golan and East Jerusalem? Was it not grotesque to see Turkey (allied with Greece!) waxing indignant over the annexation of Kuwait while, having lately ravaged Cyprus without a murmur from the West, it declared the necessity for a war to establish democracy — in Iraq!

Who will believe that there will be any attempt to force Israel to retreat from the occupied and annexed territories now that its military superiority has been restored? For fifty years the principal victims of Western politics in the region have been the Palestinian people, not Israel. Supported by the United States and Europe — unconditionally and massively, financially and militarily — Israel has been able to replay in the twentieth century the history of colonial conquest in the nineteenth. With all the arrogance that Western support has made possible, Israel has almost daily assaulted the Arab peoples, has bombed with impunity the Libyans, the Tunisians, the Iraqis.

But one can always find excuses. Israel is "democratic." Shamir is legally elected. When the victims of Zionism actively resist their exterminators, we hear a throng of courageous statesmen wax indignant and endorse further Israeli expansionism. Is it a figment of the Arab imagination that public opinion in the United States and Europe sidesteps "the Arab problem" in this shameful manner?

The Western media bombard the public with denunciations of the "religious fanaticism" of Arabs and Muslims, but few of them dare to denounce Saudi Arabia for financing these movements of despair. Let us therefore leave the propaganda and half-truths to the politicians of the United States and Europe, who must hide their power politics. Let us get on to serious matters, that is to say, to the analysis of the real stakes of the North-South conflict and their tragic expression in the Gulf War.

Actually Existing Capitalism and the Zone of Storms

The North-South conflict is the fundamental conflict of what I call "actually existing capitalism." Capitalism on a world scale, which for the five or so centuries since its origin has been polarizing the world, is responsible for the North-South split. This polarization creates misery for the popular classes in the periphery, for the majority of humanity. Growing misery, contempt for national rights, lack of democracy, all are implied by the accumulation of capital on a world scale. Under such conditions the expression that the Chinese have for the Third World, the "zone of storms," is the *mot juste,* and not merely for the moment. To be sure, the storms are not perpetual, but they are recurrent, and mark the whole history of capitalism.

It is often said that the course of the last forty years of North-South conflict has been overshadowed by the East-West conflict. But what were the Russian and Chinese revolutions but revolts of peoples on the peripheries, whose social, economic, and political conditions under capitalism were unbearable? The revolutions of Russia, China, Cuba, and Vietnam belonged to the same family as the national liberation movements in the Third World, save that the socialist revolutions, of all the popular movements on the periphery of capitalism, were the most radical, and therefore the most dangerous to capital.

Certainly the evolution of the Soviet Union after the Second World War, its accession to the status of military superpower, moved its international relations out of the realm of those typical of the North and South. These changes were, on the whole, favourable to the emancipation of the Third World, however partial.

Has the page of history been turned back? Yes, in the short run, since the U.S.S.R. has clearly indicated its intention to rejoin the Western camp. But it has only been turned back provisionally. Capitalism cannot resolve any of the fundamental social problems of the countries of the East. Some of them already suffer the scourge of peripheralization in the capitalist world system.

From the viewpoint of the fundamental conflict of actually existing capitalism, the conflict between Western capital and the peoples of the periphery, the 1980s were a period of reversals for the Third World, marked first of all by the crumbling and then by the collapse of tentative radical nationalism of the Nasserist type, which had grown up in the 1950s and 1960s. At the same time a portion of the left in the West was won over by the neo-liberal politics of followers of Reagan, Thatcher, and company. And last but not least, there was the collapse of the communists regimes of Eastern Europe and the Soviet Union. Under these conditions, we witnessed, in the last half of the 1980s, an enormous intensification of international capital's offensive aimed at restoring comprador rule in the Third World, that is, at subordinating third-world political and economic systems to the logic of the expansion of capital. The retrenchment programs imposed by the International Monetary Fund and the World Bank were linked to this offensive. The Gulf War was its most recent act of violence, though certainly not its first: it was preceded by the contra war in Nicaragua; the intervention in Grenada; the intervention in Panama (certainly complicated by the character of Noriega, but clearly aimed at protecting U.S. interests in a region it regards as its own property); numerous interventions (principally French) aimed at propping up African heads of state not well-known for their democratic tendencies. We have, therefore, been living in a period in which the suppression of the Third World has been functioning normally.

Then suddenly things exploded. Recall our point of departure: it was not the personality of Saddam Hussein or the character of his regime that was essential. At issue was control of the oil of the Arab world. The petroleum countries of the Gulf now know that they cannot exist as independent states except under the direct and permanent protection of the armies of the West. But this signifies the eventual collapse of the whole archaic system, because the military occupation cannot last forever. In this case, the Gulf crisis is a North-South Crisis. It heralds other such crises; it is only a question of time and chance. We have already seen an embryonic form in the hunger strikes against IMF "conditionalities." One place or another, these revolts against the unbearable order of world capitalism will crystallize in a new stage of struggle of the peoples of the South.

May one speak, as I have done, of "the South" in the singular? Certainly the South does not comprise a homogeneous world. It never has. It is a peculiarity of the uneven expansion of capital to homogenize its centre while it differentiates indefinitely its peripheries. The new differentiations that appeared in the Third World in the 1970s and 1980s — the semi-industrialization of some, the "fourth worldization" of others — do not at all constitute a new phenomenon, but the new form of a permanent feature of capitalist expansion. And if, from the Industrial Revolution up until the Second World War, the centre-periphery polarization essentially corresponded to the general distinction between industrial and nonindustrial countries, since that war it has not. The unequal industrialization of the Third World is the new form of world polarization; and the new form of domination of the centre over the industrialized peripheries now operates through systems of international finance, technology, and communication. In one sense it is necessary to speak of the periphery in the plural, to resist the naive temptation to reduce it all to a common denominator of analogous social formations. But one can nonetheless speak of it in the singular in the sense that there is truly a fundamental conflict between the popular masses of all the peripheries, whether semi-industrial or nonindustrial, and the logic of the world capitalist system. It may even be that this conflict is more intense and violent for the semi-industrial regions than it is for the most poverty-stricken.

The Third World, then, is a "zone of storms." In light of this fact, after the Second World War, the West (the United States, Canada, Australia, Western Europe, Israel, Japan) arrayed a panoply of means to assure its solidarity and to marshal its common strategies: the OECD and the EEC on the economic level, the Council of Europe and the Trilateral Commission on the political level, NATO on the military level. Ostensibly put in place to confront communism, these institutions have been the guarantors of an international status quo favourable to imperialist domination. Far from rendering these institutions obsolete, the East-West rapprochement has given them a second life vis-à-vis the peoples of the Third World. The unification of the world by the market will not lead to peace, but on the contrary to the intensification of storms of violence against the victims of the market.

At the present — on the occasion of the crisis — we are even seeing the reappearance of the old U.S.-European project of a "regional military pact" among the comprador regimes of the Gulf regions (it was called

CENTO in the 1950s and 1960s), inviting the West to guarantee the status quo, prolonging the life of NATO by giving apparent legitimacy to Western interventions to put down revolts of the people. One recalls that CENTO was billed as "anti-Soviet," while its imperialist dimension was masked by anti-communist rhetoric. For all that, the CENTO project has resurfaced just as the U.S.S.R. has ceased to be an enemy!

An Alternative European Perspective?

The Gulf conflict has tragically revealed the limits of an "alternative European perspective" on the world order, detached from the Atlantic alignment. The European absence from the Gulf conflict was predictable. The description of Germany as an "economic giant and political dwarf," might now be applied to all of Europe. England put itself in fundamental conflict with any genuinely European perspective when it decided in 1945 to become a junior partner of the United States. Germany, for its part, has no specific interest in the South for now. It is preoccupied with its expansion to the East, and otherwise follows the lead of the United States. France, Italy, and Spain, the weaker nations of Europe, are marginalized by their impotence.

The coup that the United States has carried off in the Gulf will be a challenge to the Europeans. It is clear that the U.S. will use its military control over the oil of the Gulf to impose its politics on Europe. It is necessary, therefore, for the Europeans to develop a long-term political strategy to take account of these new givens — to strive to build a newly unified Europe "from the Atlantic to the Urals," to use a phrase of DeGaulle's, or a "common home," to echo Gorbachev's words. This perspective must get the support of progressive and democratic forces if Europe is to be able to face the problems of the Arab world and the South in general.

Does responsibility for the present European dilemma fall on Gorbachev's pro-Western turn? It is not certain. If the Europeans, specifically the French, had adopted a stronger position, daring to confront the United States, it is probable that the Soviets and Chinese would have followed. For, though Gorbachev lacked the power to confront the United States and Europe simultaneously, he might have had a different attitude if he had the support of Europe. If France had not withdrawn its proposal for a negotiated solution before the Security Council on the 14th of January, there would have been a veto but the United States and England would have been isolated.

Things being what they are, however, will the Gulf War lead to a resumption of U.S. hegemony? I do not think so. In fact, the war may consolidate a triumvirate — the United States, Japan, Germany. The latter two countries, which contributed heavily to the financing of the war, know how to pay America to police a world unified by the market. Along with this group, I see weaker countries like the U.S.S.R., marginalized countries like France, comprador countries like the majority of the states of the Third World. This new order hardly merits a name of its own; I call it the Empire of Disorder, structured by a strictly military self-concept, without any vision that would enable it to address the genuine problems of humanity.

The Gulf War, therefore, has not really changed the world order; it has prolonged the capitalist order. In order to bring this order to an end, it is necessary to refuse the one-sided logic of neo-liberalism, to place politics in command, and to begin to construct a polycentric world system capable of solving the problems of interdependence on a planetary scale and flexible enough to allow autonomy to the separate regions.

A related question concerns the role of the United Nations. Until now, the U.N. system has not functioned as foreseen in its charter. In effect, the United Nations has been paralysed by the domination of the West; by the fact that the Third World has only functioned in this system at the level of rhetoric. The United Nations has never been able to advance any cause favouring the people of the Third World against the wishes of the West.

Can we create a positive role for the United Nations? The Gulf crisis should make us wary. For there is always the brutal and predictable response of the United States, which will put itself forward as an international policeman to pursue its own purposes. The Gulf War delivered a severe blow to the chances that the end of the Cold War would permit the UN to start building a genuinely peaceful world.

Polycentrism and Progressive Social Transformation

There is an alternative to the disastrous politics in which the dominant powers of the West have ensnared the world. I have in mind an ideal world that has a really polycentric basis for its politics, that comprises on the one hand the unity of European economics and politics and on the other an Arab unity accompanied by gradual integration of the Arab states. These two regions could both benefit from autonomy relative to the United Sates. Arab unity is an essential condition for a solution to the problems of the regions, but a solution of these problems is in turn a condition of positive North-South cooperation, European and Arab.

This vision conflicts with the dominant vision in the West. Europe does not yet accept the idea of Arab unity, and always refers to it as a danger. To be sure, it is not the order of the day. Certainly the powers that be in the Arab states, compradors that they are, cannot countenance unity. It is clear that the way to Arab unity — an undeniable requirement for solving the problems of the Arab peoples, which have the highest priority of our epoch — is a long and convoluted path. It is impossible to conceive of Arab unity today as German unity could be conceived of in the 19th century, as achievable through conquest. The mistake of a dictator like Saddam Hussein is to fail to comprehend this. The sole path is that of democracy, of progressive social transformations, of respect for the diversity of local interests. This way is not really utopian. It is less so than European unity, which is hampered by Europe's lack of the cultural and linguistic unity that characterizes the Arabs.

A truly polycentric world necessarily implies regional structures of this type, not solely in the Arab world, but elsewhere in the Third World, in Africa, for example. But European politics are remarkably bad in this respect. France particularly, but also Italy and Spain, nurse the notion of "breaking" Arab unity by offering the ruling classes of the Maghreb the prospect of hitching themselves to the European train.

In fact, the hostility of Europe to Arab unity is the product of its Atlantic perspective, and of its support for the expansionist objectives of Zionism. The United States and Israel see that their interests lie in Arab weakness. The Europeans do not distinguish their interests from these. This attitude tends to snowball, because the Arab response — the spontaneous reaction of the masses, Islamist manipulations, disavowal of moderate Arab diplomatic efforts — nourish an anti-Arab discourse to the exclusive benefit of the United States and Israel.

For thirty years the United States has stirred up its allies and clients against the menace of the East. Today they use the revolts of peoples of the South as a pretext to victimize them further. All the democracies that sincerely want a genuinely new world order ought openly to disavow this United States. Unless he is challenged, Mr. Bush will continue, after the Gulf War as after the invasions of Grenada and Panama, to police the world and impose on it an order "made in America."

Part II

Whither the Revolutions?

Chapter Four

Central America In Transition: Between An Imperial Past And An Uncertain Future*

Susanne Jonas

Many observers now argue that Central America has reached the "end of the revolutionary cycle": and is slipping back into its traditional subordination to the United States. Events since late 1989, beginning with the U.S. invasion of Panama and the electoral defeat of the Sandinistas in Nicaragua, seem to confirm this view — all the more so in the wake of the 1991 U.S. military victory in the Persian Gulf War. But from a longer-range perspective, the future is less determined and the balance is less one-sided than might at first appear. Following two decades of upheaval and resistance before the Sandinista triumph in 1979, the struggles of the 1980s have seen both advances and setbacks. They have extracted a painfully high toll in human lives — over 200,000 have been killed in Nicaragua, El Salvador and Guatemala. But despite these costs, I shall argue, the revolutionary processes of the 1980s have permanently transformed the region and its people, and they can be expected to continue into the future, albeit in new forms and on new terms. Given that the civil wars in Nicaragua, El Salvador and Guatemala are being ended through negotiations rather than defeat of the revolutionary forces, the region will never again be simply the "backyard" of the United States.

---

* This chapter is a revised and updated version of an article published in *Monthly Review*, Vol. 42, No. 2 (June 1990)

Although there can be no "return" to the pre-1980s past, the 1990s will certainly pose new challenges. Especially in view of massive and rapid changes in the international environment, it will be a time of great uncertainty, and will doubtless bring new troubles to Central America. The bankruptcy of the existing order is evident (for example, in the economic disaster throughout the region); but the forms and objectives of struggles to change it are by no means clear. The outcome of those struggles will depend largely on the ability of popular and revolutionary movements to project a new vision and develop alternative strategies to neo-liberal economics and counterinsurgency politics.

Nicaragua, El Salvador, Guatemala

In Nicaragua, the people carried out a revolution and survived nine years of unrelenting U.S. attack. Eventually, however, through its devastating military and economic war, the United States was able to raise the cost to an intolerable level, and thus to achieve its goal of ousting the Sandinistas from state power. The material achievements of the Revolution were limited from the start, and some were completely reversed, by the U.S. determination to turn a positive example into a negative example (primarily through the contra war); but other aspects of the Revolution were institutionalized in the 1987 Constitution, and cannot be rolled back without further violence. Further, the Sandinistas laid the bases for a profound democratization of Nicaraguan society — its political culture as well as its institutions — and undertook a unique experiment in revolutionary pluralism, based on a multi-party system and integrating representative with popular/participatory democracy. They carried forward Nicaragua's historical traditions and in many respects took the only road open to them, given international conditions in the 1980s. This is not to minimize the many errors they made in areas where they did have choices — errors which only began to be examined after February 1990.

The defeat of the Sandinistas in the 1990 election, held under siege, was not itself a catastrophic turnaround (as was the 1973 Chilean coup or the 1954 "liberation" of Guatemala); it accentuated trends that were already in motion. Viewed in its totality, the Nicaraguan experience of the 1980s demonstrated that peace could only be achieved (the contra war could only be ended) through *concertacion* or political agreement. Particularly after the beginning of the Central American Peace Process in 1987, the Sandinistas had already made significant concessions to the civilian opposition; even if they had won the 1990 election, they would have had to reach further agreements, even to "share power" in some respects. Conversely, even in opposition, the Sandinistas and popular social movements remain the most powerful political force in the country, certainly strong enough to continue the democratization of Nicaraguan society and compel de facto power-sharing by Union Nacional de Oposicion (UNO) if the United States does not prevent it. The only alternative to power-sharing will be a renewal of civil war.

At the same time, economic conditions in post-Sandinista Nicaragua are more devastating than ever for the popular classes; skyrocketing inflation, aggravated by the removal of the social supports established during the Sandinista era, leave many people in desperate straits. For the moment, UNO's inability to correct the economic situation creates great discontent with the government and appears to favour the Sandinistas; but this cannot be taken for granted long-range, as popular discontent could turn into apathy or cynicism. In order to address this situation, the Sandinistas face formidable tasks. Beyond preserving their unity, they must satisfy the demands of their popular base, where people are not necessarily willing to go along with what they perceive as a "deal" worked out at the top between the Frente Sandinista de Liberation Nacional (FSLN) leadership and UNO. The FSLN must walk a very fine line, addressing those demands and fighting against further anti-popular measures, but without provoking a total crisis for UNO "moderates" who have been willing to negotiate with them. Most urgently, the Sandinistas will have to project a clear direction for their party (both electoral and mobilizational) and to offer clear alternatives to neo-liberal economic policies.

Beyond Nicaragua, the entire region has been undergoing profound structural transformations and political upheavals. The Central American countries have been shaken by several economic crises: first, the land crisis in the countryside, resulting from the expansion of capitalist export agriculture and a new wave of expropriations of peasants; second, following the oil shocks of 1973 and 1979 and the plummeting of prices for their basic exports, a generalized depression throughout the 1980s, comparable in magnitude and gravity to that of the 1930s. These crises have caused massive population dislocations, and have regenerated social inequalities far too profound to be resolved by existing regimes. In El Salvador and Guatemala, these have exploded into prolonged civil wars, with the established regimes facing serious challenges from popular and revolutionary forces.

In both countries, popular forces have proven surprisingly resilient through the decade, despite massive repression; for their part, the revolutionary movements have shown considerable ability to learn from their mistakes and increasing flexibility in redefining their goals in accordance with new domestic and international realities — specifically, in pressing for negotiated settlements to the long civil wars. This has given them increasing legitimacy, relative to their situation in 1980.

In El Salvador, from nearly all sectors of society, there has been strong pressure for a just settlement of the war in the late 1980s, challenging the determination of the United States, the army and the oligarchy *not* to negotiate. The November 1989 Frente Farabundo Marti para la Liberación Nacional (FMLN) offensive was designed, above all, to demonstrate the need for serious negotiations. One long-range consequence of the offensive may have been the emergence of a sector of the Salvadoran bourgeoisie that prefers negotiations to further destruction of the economy (i.e., their property) through more war. There may even be some army officers who favour negotiations, but they will come forward only if the United States changes its longstanding opposition. These complex dynamics have become clear in the government-FMLN negotiations that ran the course of 1990 and continued into 1991. Despite periodic escalations of the war, the negotiation *process* was maintained; however, it has remained deadlocked on the central issue of restructuring the armed forces, on which both the Salvadoran government and the U.S. government have refused to make concessions.

In early 1990 the head of the U.S. Southern Command acknowledged publicly that the FMLN could not be militarily defeated; nevertheless, the United States did not depart radically from its prior policy of prosecuting the war to defeat the FMLN, rather than ending it through negotiations. In the fall of 1990, the Bush administration was forced to comply with congressional cuts in military aid to El Salvador; but it took the first available opportunity in January 1991 (under cover of the Persian Gulf War) to restore the aid. Subsequently, while verbally recognizing the need for negotiations with the FMLN, Washington has maintained a hardline position, opposing U.N. proposals and refusing to accept real concessions on key issues.

By the late 1980s, meanwhile, the FMLN had learned the "lessons of Nicaragua": watching the destruction of Nicaragua through military and economic war during the 1980s (even before the 1990 Nicaraguan election) contributed to a gradual change of FMLN strategy from "taking power" to gaining a share of power. Washington had made clear, even under Carter, that it would not permit "another Nicaragua" (another revolutionary victory); and Reagan policy demonstrated the U.S. ability to punish (destroy) Nicaragua. "Taking state power" outright became unfeasible, and revolutionaries in El Salvador (and Guatemala) learned to seek other routes for realizing popular demands — negotiations, power-sharing, grassroots mobilizations, even competing for power in elections (if their integrity could be guaranteed) — while continuing miliary action. At the same time, these movements have redefined the relation of armed confrontations to mass-based political struggles (the latter no longer an instrument of the former), and the role of democratic demands.

Guatemala has sustained the hemisphere's longest and bloodiest insurgency/counterinsurgency, a *thirty-year war,* costing 200,000 lives since 1960. In the last two decades, the guerrilla movement made a major advance over the limited and flawed *foco* strategy of the 1960s,[1] when it began to address demands of ethnic identity as well as class and to put the concerns of the country's Indian majority at the centre of the revolutionary struggle. Nevertheless, the massive uprising of the late 1970s and early 1980s in the Indian highlands suffered a major defeat as a result of the genocidal army response of 1981-83, wiping 440 villages off the face of the map, and killing over 100,000 unarmed civilians. By the late 1980s, the revolutionary movement Unidad Revolucionaria Nacional de Guatemala (URNG) recovered from this defeat and once again has taken political and military initiatives, while popular organizations have engaged in a slow, difficult rebuilding process. The civil war in Guatemala remains the hardest to end; its continuation will affect the region as a whole.

By 1990-91, that war was intensifying, but with important departures from the previous 30 years. For some time, the URNG has recognized that it cannot "take state power" militarily, and that, in any case, the cost of pursuing such a strategy would be too high. Hence, the URNG has been pressing for negotiations since the return of civilian government in 1986. For years, the government stubbornly insisted that the insurgents must simply "lay down their arms." But during the course of 1990 and in early 1991, even government and army spokesmen (as well as the private sector, whose properties were increasingly affected) were finally forced to acknowledge the significant upsurge in guerrilla capabilities. This implicit admission that the war could not be "won" militarily created the conditions, for the first time beginning in the spring of 1990, for discussions about ending the war. The year 1990 saw a broad-based National Dialogue process involving virtually all sectors of Guatemalan society except the government and army; and in the spring of 1991, even they finally recognized the need to begin a serious negotiation process, dropping the precondition that the guerrillas first disarm. Doubtless, that process carries very high risks as well as great hopes, since it is staunchly opposed by the civilian and military ultra-Right; it promises to be arduous and prolonged, with sudden ups and downs; it will be accompanied by continuing violence, and will likely include periodic escalations of the war. Nevertheless, this process is the terrain on which the battle for Guatemala's future will be fought in coming years.

The Central American Peace Process

At the regional level, the Central American Peace Process that began in mid-1987 initially appeared to open up an alternative to the decades of war; and for a brief moment, political solutions to these wars seemed possible. By negotiating with the contras, Nicaragua provided an impressive example of what the political will for peace could accomplish. Together with the broad opposition within the United States to interventionism in Central America, the Peace Process finally forced the Reagan administration, against its will, to end contra military aid.

Nevertheless, within a year, the initially high hopes for peace were greatly reduced, as the United States reasserted its ability, if not to control the future of Central America directly, at least to prevent demobilization of the contras. Meanwhile, the four pro-U.S. governments refused to apply the Accords in their own countries. In 1988-89, their already-tenuous commitment to peaceful coexistence was undermined by a trend toward the Right, beginning with the March 1989 victory of the hardline anti-Nicaragua Alianza Republicana Nacionalista (ARENA) in El Salvador. By the time of the December 1989 Presidents' meeting, the process became an instrument for legitimating the ARENA government in El Salvador.

The positive potential of the Peace Process was greatly limited, in the end, because Central America is considered by the United States to be within its direct sphere of influence, and is probably the last region of the world where the United States will make concessions. As of 1990-91, regional diplomacy no longer represents a genuine peace process or an exercise in relative autonomy from the United States. Future progress toward regional autonomy will require changes within these countries. But for the moment, with the Sandinistas out of power in Nicaragua, the existing rightist governments have little reason to pressure each other for negotiations or democratization.

If there should be a negotiated settlement in El Salvador — which appears more possible than previously — it would constitute a serious pressure for such a solution in Guatemala. (Indeed, El Salvador is an "easier" case than Guatemala insofar as the war has not been as long, and the army is less entrenched and less powerful relative to the insurgency.) However, if this does not happen soon, El Salvador could come to resemble Guatemala. This could even include a last-ditch effort by Salvadoran hardliners to implement the "Guatemala solution," a total war, with massive casualties within a few months. Further, El Salvador continues to be affected by the situation in Guatemala — as shown by the January 1990 murder in Guatemala of Salvadoran social democratic leader Hector Oqueli, which involved Guatemala's security forces and death squads at least indirectly.

Sooner or later, proponents of peace and democracy in the region will have to confront the Guatemalan counterinsurgency state. Meanwhile, the continuation of war in Guatemala affects the region as a whole.

The other great negative factor within the region is the economic crisis, which has brought negative growth rates and has driven living standards down to the level of 17 years ago. In some countries, over 85 percent of the population now lives in poverty; inflation and unemployment continue to skyrocket, leaving many with no option but to migrate North. The medicine for these ills has made the patients worse: structural adjustment programs and harsh neo-liberal policies have had disastrous effects for the popular classes. Less regressive alternatives to neo-liberalism, including the recomposition of the Central American Common Market on the basis of reformist policies that would expand the domestic market as well as new exports, appear unviable for the moment. Such proposals lack sufficient financial resources from their supporters in the United Nations and Western Europe, and are opposed by the United States and the major lending agencies (International Monetary Fund, World Bank).

Yet these negative factors have regenerated popular protest and maintained Central America as a zone of upheaval and challenge to the United States. Indeed, many of the very contradictions that produced the Nicaraguan Revolution have deepened, since the 1980s brought greater inequalities and economic crisis, not growth. The continuation of protest does not by itself imply new victories; but the revolutionary processes are likely to continue into the forseeable future, both in traditional forms (if necessary) and in new forms.

The Hemispheric Context

Within the broader Latin American context, the balance is also mixed. On the one hand, significant and unprecedented advances (near-victories in the late 1980s) for popular and leftist forces in Brazil and Mexico portend the possible spread of "democratic" models (electoral/obilizational, both inside and outside the electoral system) for far-eaching social change on the continent. In Mexico, the challenge to one-party rule by the Partido Revolucionario Institucional (PRI), and in Brazil, the prospect of replacing 25 years of military dictatorship and counterinsurgency politics with broad-based popular politics, represented important steps forward. Although their advances remain slow and uneven, difficult to sustain, and thus far programmatically weak, broad popular left blocs are likely to emerge in a number of countries.

On the other hand, there are two overwhelmingly negative factors. The first is Latin America's structural impoverishment. By almost all indicators, according to the United Nations and the Inter-American Development Bank, the standard of living in Latin America is much lower today than 10 years ago, and there is no indication that this tendency will be reversed. Further, the economic crisis of the 1980s ended the era of growth for nearly all Latin American economies. The debt crisis has left virtually all countries dependent on the International Monetary Fund (IMF), but neo-liberal IMF policies have seriously aggravated the social crises. Neo-liberal dogma is running rampant: for example, although the June 1990 defeat of Vargas Llosa in Peru demonstrated popular rejection of such policies, winner Fujimori has implemented an even more extreme version. U.S. economic initiatives (the Bush "Enterprise for the Americas" and North American Common Market plans) dominate the economic agenda. Meanwhile, genuine economic alternatives for Latin America which combine growth with social equity and ecological considerations, which seek to define a more favourable relation to the world market — and *which must be regional in scope* — remain to be defined in concrete proposals.

The second negative development is the resurgence of overt U.S. interventionism in the hemisphere, as seen in the invasion of Panama and stepped up U.S. military operations in the drug wars. Such interventionism has generated nationalist responses from broad sectors of Latin American society and from some governments, but the latter have been so weakened by economic collapse that their protestations are mainly verbal (e.g., after the invasion of Panama). These assertions of "relative autonomy" vis-à-vis the United States echo earlier expressions (e.g., the Contadora initiative and proposals to reincorporate Cuba into the Inter-American system). Such expressions will likely continue — the clock cannot be turned back to 1965, when the Organization of American States (OAS) sent troops to support the U.S. invasion of the Dominican Republic, — but thus far their impact remains quite relative.

The other main target of U.S. interventionism is Cuba. Almost uninterruptedly since 1959, U.S. policy has been governed by an obsession with Cuba that has made "new thinking" almost impossible, especially toward Central America and the Caribbean. U.S. triumphalism over victories in Panama, Nicaragua, and the Persian Gulf could make the 1990s particularly dangerous for Cuba. The future of Cuba will depend primarily upon the ability of the Cuban government and society to respond to internal crisis; but at the same time, there are ominous signs that the United States sees an opportunity to "go for broke," to reclaim the entire hemisphere again by destabilizing the Cuban government. If such efforts were to succeed, the impact for Latin America would be devastating.

Central America in the New International Disorder

Internationally, the end of the 1980s initiated an era of profound and unexpectedly rapid restructuring including the "end of the Cold War" and perestroika in the socialist world. In addition to reducing East-West tensions, these changes initially held out hopes for negotiated solutions to long-standing regional conflicts. In principle, the "end of the Cold War" removed the communist/socialist "enemy" and hence the basis for rigid, Manichaean anti-communist thinking in the United States, and laid the basis for de-escalation of conflicts in regions where the Soviet Union could actively advance peace. The realities of Soviet internal crisis and international weakness have subsequently vitiated the potential for a major Soviet role in the Third World. Combined with economic changes in the international capitalist economy that further impoverish most areas of the Third World, the new conjuncture leaves progressives in the Third World with fewer options than ever.

For Central America, at least in the short run, these changes reduce the margins of manoeuvre or "relative autonomy" vis-à-vis the major external power, the United States, and leave uncertain prospects for peace. In this case, peace would require an evolution in the thinking of U.S. policymakers as profound as that which initially occurred in the Soviet Union. Such "new thinking" in Washington would imply abandoning all the premises of the Cold War and redefining "U.S. interests," it would have to include a recognition of the *structural* (not "communist") roots of revolutionary movements in Central America, and the reality and legitimacy of popular struggles for social justice. Thus far, rather than any such evolution in the mentality of Washington policymakers, there has been a hardening of U.S. interventionism in the hemisphere and a continued adherence to basic assumptions of the geopolitical, "East-West" mentality. (For example, even after the Sandinistas accepted their electoral defeat and peacefully transferred power to UNO, the United States has continued to pressure for their removal from all positions of power, in part on the basis of a "domino theory" assumption that their presence feeds the FMLN insurgency in El Salvador. Another example is the hardening U.S. line against Cuba.)

But *the world is changing,* at a pace and in ways previously unimagined. U.S. economic power world-wide is undergoing a relative decline — even if that fact is virtually obscured by the stunning U.S. military victory in the Persian Gulf. And even though the U.S. military triumph portends a "Pax Americana" in the immediate future, the longer-range social and political contradictions and destabilizing consequences of U.S. actions may frustrate U.S. objectives. In the words of Carlos Fuentes after the U.S. invasion of Panama, "We Latin Americans should always remember that the world no longer reacts to the provincial visions or illusions of the United States. The mechanisms of change that have been set into motion are too profound, even if their results are as yet unforeseeable." From this perspective, we should not discard the possibility that the United States and its counter-insurgent allies could eventually be forced to negotiate an end to the wars in Central America and to permit initiatives by popular forces in other Latin countries. Certainly, this is difficult to envision; but the United States does face objective constraints on its ability to control Latin America (budgetary limits, other international priorities, etc.).

More immediately, however, the United States has responded to international changes by reinforcing its "natural" sphere of influence in this hemisphere. To the extent that U.S.-Soviet agreements remove important restraints on U.S. intervention in the Third World, the new global order (or disorder) could be even more dangerous. Minimally, the Soviet Union's commitment to domestic priorities in the face of massive internal crisis implies pulling back farther than previously from support of Third World struggles. At the same time, Western European governments — which during the 1980s supported regional negotiations and human rights, and generally served as a counterweight to U.S. policies in Central America — have greatly lowered their profile in the region; they are unlikely to contribute significant material resources to Central America, in view of growing economic relations with Eastern Europe. This leaves the future of Central America primarily in the hands of the United States and the IMF, which are thoroughly committed to neo-liberal policies.

Even before the Persian Gulf War, there were indicators of increasing U.S. interventionism in the Third World. As seen in key policy documents,[2] U.S. policymakers envision more rather than less armed confrontation with Third World "enemies" (Marxist-Leninists, terrorists, drug-traffickers, etc.), and see a need to defeat such enemies "decisively and rapidly." The Pentagon also reaffirmed its conviction that the "Soviet threat" remains undiminished in the Third World, and that the United States should continue to back "freedom fighters" and use military power in the Third World. This is compounded by an almost messianic mentality in U.S. policy circles and among policy intellectuals (Brzezinski, untington, et al.), heavily reflected in the mass media, in which the contradictions of socialism are taken to demonstrate the absolute "triumph of capitalism" — while the absolute immiseration of the Third World, which is an integral part of world *capitalism*, is totally ignored.

At the same time, another great restraint upon U.S. intervention in the Third World has been decisively weakened: opposition to such interventions from American public opinion (the "Vietnam Syndrome"). Throughout the 1980s, the United States was prevented from directly invading Central America by lack of public support; opinion polls from 1979 on showed consistently that over two thirds of the American public opposed interventionist policies in Central America, even when conducted by a very popular President, and even when phrased in terms of "stopping Communism." It was for this reason that the Reagan administration had to channel funds to the contras illegally (hence the Contragate scandal).

The Bush administration, which in many respects continued Reagan policy in Central America, understood the imperative of overcoming this great weakness of Reagan's contra policy, its lack of support from Congress and from the American public. (On other Central America issues, most Democrats had been compliant since 1984.) Bush and Secretary of State James Baker used the March 1989 "bipartisan accord" with Congressional Democrats to repair the Contragate damage and obtain a virtual green light for interventionism in Central America (continued "humanitarian" aid to the contras, economic war against Nicaragua, and counterinsurgency assistance to Guatemala and El Salvador). And with the invasion of Panama in December 1989, neither Congressional Democrats nor the U.S. public objected even to direct involvement of U.S. troops, so long as such involvement was "successful," and not prolonged or costly in U.S. lives. If there was any doubt about this after Panama, it appears to have been erased by domestic responses to the Persian Gulf War.

This very negative development is perhaps an expression of what Fred Halliday has identified as a "quasi-totalitarian" anti-internationalist, anti-Third World political culture running rampant throughout the advanced capitalist world. In the United States, this trend can conceivably be counter-balanced in the 1990s only by the revival of mass-based popular movements, particularly for the rights of women and people of colour — and by the birth of a new political culture growing out of those movements, internationalist as well as egalitarian in its outlook.

The problem of U.S. power in Central America is in large measure the problem of how the dominant class maintains its grip over American public opinion. (Samir Amin recently referred to the role of the mass media in this regard as an ideological "carpet bombing of public consciousness.") The anti-intervention movement in the United States played an important role in defeating military aid to the contras, but was never able to force an open debate about the devastating economic war that destroyed Nicaragua. It was ineffective in the face of jingoistic justifications of the assault on Panama. While church-based and other forces mobilized significant public pressure against military aid to El Salvador, they have not yet effectively confronted the Bush administration's very deliberate policy of "overcoming" the Vietnam Syndrome and reconstructing the "bipartisan consensus" in regard to Central America.

By the early 1990s, a revival of broad-based movements in the United States seems possible, especially among women and minority communities. In principle, the end of the Cold War has created space for demanding a "peace dividend" for communities ridden with poverty, joblessness, homelessness, and drugs — problems of particular concern to people of colour and women. It also created space for challenging a "bipartisan consensus" based on outmoded Cold War ideologies in areas like Central America. But all of these potential openings within the United States are in danger of being closed, in the wake of the Persian Gulf War and the likelihood of further U.S. military interventions in the Third World.

To summarize: The "post-Cold War" order is not necessarily the opposite of the Cold War in the Third World (i.e., peace), but rather a highly volatile transition period, whose outcome is uncertain. The most negative factors are structural immiseration (aggravated by neo-liberal policies), and the decreasing international restraints upon U.S. interventionism, at least in the short run. For Central America, the most positive factors are still those on the ground. If anything can stay the hand of intervention, and challenge its creation, the counterinsurgency state, it is most likely to be some combination of popular/revolutionary forces which accumulated strength and a great deal of political learning during the 1980s. These forces are not strong enough to triumph outright, but they are too strong to be defeated or discounted. The immediate future looks very difficult for the popular classes in Central America; but longer-range, the contradictions of structural crisis and U.S. intervention could favour popular/revolutionary forces in those countries where they are well organized, broadly based and able to develop strategies appropriate for new conditions. Perhaps we can dare to hope that the prolongation of the Central American struggles into the next decade will bring concrete gains and, within a very difficult international environment, expand the limits of the "possible."

Notes

1. Editors' Note: "*Foquismo* was a strategy of irregular warfare leading to popular insurrection, with the 'subjective conditions' being created by the exemplary actions of a revolutionary vanguard; the guerrilla center of operations was designed to politicize the local population, to create 'liberated zones' in the countryside, and eventually build enough support to lay the basis for taking power." Susanne Jonas, *The Battle for Guatemala*. Boulder, CO: Westview Press, 1991, p. 67.
2. For example, "Discriminate Deterrence," a high-level bi-partisan recommendation in 1988 for more security/counterinsurgency assistance with fewer restrictions, and subsequently, a Bush administration national security review.

Chapter Five

U.S. Imperialism and Nicaragua: Did the Contras Lose the War But Win the Election?

David Close

Many who supported Sandinista Nicaragua likely attribute the Frente's 1990 electoral loss to U.S. imperialism. It is not hard to understand why. Just looking at the campaign provides plenty of evidence. The U.S. government ignored treaties among the Central Americans that called for the contras to demobilize, disarm and return to Nicaragua well before the vote. Instead, the contras were more active militarily during the campaign than they had been for two years. And a lot of U.S. money, $26 million according to one calculation,[1] went to back what had been a shaky alignment of opposition parties — the Union Nacional de Oposicion (UNO). Even the make-up of UNO, with its heavy reliance on Nicaragua's ultra-right, reflects the hand of Washington.

Obviously, Washington's ten-year plan to destroy the revolution through a combination of counterrevolutionary war, diplomatic pressure, and an economic embargo influenced the election's outcome, but to conclude that this meant the Sandinistas never had a chance goes too far for two reasons. First, it absolves the Frente Sandinista de Liberacion Nacional (FSLN) from responsibility for errors it made in government and during the campaign, thus heightening the chances that the same mistakes will be repeated. The more important reason, however, is that it makes imperialism appear invincible.

If the White House and its minions were the preordained victors in their contest with the revolutionary state, the whole Sandinista experiment was a waste of lives and wealth. Indeed, any radical political project would be doomed from the moment the United States, or other imperialist power, decided it had to go. But if the FSLN is responsible for its loss — if it could have won by doing some things differently, Washington's designs might have been frustrated. The contras could have lost both the war and the elections, and the sacrifices and suffering of untold Nicaraguans would have been justified.

I believe that examining the election closely will show that the Frente's loss was not inevitable. We must consider the logic of the Sandinista project, the nature of the counterrevolution and the immediate causes of the 1990 electoral defeat. Only by grasping the dynamics of both U.S. policy toward Nicaragua and Sandinista political practice can we understand both what happened and how to keep it from happening again.

The Sandinista Project

When the Sandinistas overthrew Tacho Somoza and his family's dynastic dictatorship, they headed a multi-class alliance.[2] Having a multi-class alliance lead a revolution and take power does not mean a multi-class, pluralistic government follows, as Cuba shows. In Nicaragua, however, the FSLN included representatives of the bourgeoisie and technical strata in government, though it was careful to ensure that revolutionaries held the balance of power.[3] Along with political pluralism came a mixed economy, a foreign policy that sought relations with all countries, and tolerance toward the "non-revolutionary" classes.[4]

All of this had formed part of the Sandinistas pre-Triumph program and it reflected a mature and realistic assessment of the nature of Nicaragua. Putting these principles into practice in a revolutionary setting, however, gave political and economic pluralism different meanings than they have in a bourgeois, liberal setting. The rules of liberal democracy favouring private enterprise and encouraging citizen participation in politics only in periodic ballots were suspended. In their place came standards establishing the state as the centre of accumulation and asking the great mass of the citizenry (the popular classes) to become permanently involved in policy-making.

Creating this kind of democratic society requires policies and institutions not found in advanced capitalist democracies. Because revolutionary states want to change society thoroughly and rapidly, they normally concentrate power in the hands of one central authority. Most frequently, this authority is a vanguard party with a legal monopoly on state power. The remaining machinery of government and politics — courts, representative assemblies, interest groups and bureaucracies — is also tailored to the demands of social transformation. Practical politics in these states magnify the power of the forces of change allied with the government and systematically reduce the weight of opposing interests. Transformational politics, those of the great social revolutions from France to Nicaragua, do openly what conventional liberal politics, those of Canada or the United States, do more covertly: rig a political system so it systematically favours certain interests and produces certain outcomes.

In Sandinista Nicaragua the FSLN assumed the role of vanguard of the revolution. It built political institutions that promoted the interests of the poor and marginalized. From the privileged position accorded the Sandinista mass organizations,[5] through the pattern of representation in the quasi-legislative Council of State and on to the emphasis placed on the Area of People's Property (the state or public sector) and cooperatives in economic policy, Sandinista politics were the politics of radical social transformation.

Changes began in 1982, about the time the counterrevolutionary insurgency started to escalate. The first real sign of a new outlook was the 1983 Political Parties Law. Its original draft gave the right to govern to the Sandinistas alone, although other parties could "participate in public administration." But when finally passed, two years later, it gave any party not promoting a return to Somocismo the right to govern if it could win an election. Though of limited practical importance at first, the measure moved Nicaragua away from revolutionary vanguardism.

Over the next few years the Sandinista state and its policies became less radical. Competitive elections were held; the Council of State was abolished and replaced by the more conventional National Assembly;[6] agrarian reform titles were given to individual smallholders instead of just to members of coops; and a series of austerity drives shrank social programmes and cut thousands of public sector jobs. The contra war obviously played an important part in taking the edge off the revolution.

The perceived need to maintain national unity produced compromises with the bourgeoisie; the necessity to both protect peasants from the contras and keep their political allegiance prompted revisions in the agrarian reform law; and the financial burden of fighting Washington's paladins demanded that money be reallocated to the defence budget.

Counterrevolution and imperialism have been busy in Nicaragua; but we cannot forget that some of the policy shifts had their roots in the logic of the Sandinista project. As long as non-Sandinista, even non-revolutionary, interests and classes were part of the state structure (e.g., in the Council of State, heading a department of government, or being regularly consulted about economic matters) they had a legitimate voice in setting policy. To have denied them the right to participate in government would have broken the "civic pact" the Sandinistas concluded with more conservative anti-Somocistas and heightened domestic political conflict.[7]

Moreover, the FSLN's commitment to political pluralism made cutting deals with the opposition logical. Giving capitalists a significant role in a state-centred mixed economy let government believe policies benefitting the private sector were acceptable, even if not desirable. The options chosen under the pressure of war had long been present. Nicaragua was never Cuba: Managua's transformational model demanded less radical social restructuring than did Havana's.[8] Thus the Sandinistas did not need extensive control over the state and civil society and could let bourgeois options exist.

In opening the revolution to the right, the Sandinistas learned that liberalization is a two-edged sword. Its positive edge allows new ideas to percolate freely from all sectors of society to top decision-makers. This reminds the powerful that they are not exempt from criticism. It cuts the other way by letting foes of the regime openly promote their anti-revolutionary politics. Substantial participation and wide consultation let the FSLN minimize domestic civil conflict — the absence of any violent response to its austerity plans is evidence of this. Yet it also gave the anti-revolutionary and counterrevolutionary[9] interests room to operate.

However, we should not conclude that things would have been better had the Sandinistas been more intransigent. First, the experience of Eastern Europe shows how one-party vanguardism produces political and social sclerosis that leads to decay. Second, it is not clear that a more radical Nicaragua could have raised the foreign aid it needed to keep going; certainly the Soviets showed little interest in taking on another Cuba and western European social democrats might have been less willing to assist a more plainly Marxist regime. Third, a more obviously "communist totalitarian" Nicaragua might have invited greater U.S. pressure, perhaps even direct military intervention. Finally, we should not assume that Nicaraguans would have accepted a more restrictive regime without complaint. A more orthodox Marxist-Leninist order need not have proven any more capable of defending the revolution than was the open and pluralistic model of the Sandinistas.

Low-Intensity Conflict and Counterrevolution

Imperialism's newest weapon to combat revolution is Low-Intensity Conflict (LIC). John Saul[10] calls it a total war of attrition, more a "strategy of slow strangulation — attacking...and disrupting normal economic life (while) draining off scarce...resources...into the defence effort..." than of military conquest. Colonel John Waghelstein,[11] a leading U.S. authority on LIC, puts the military aspect of LIC fourth in importance, behind its political, economic and psychological sides. LIC's objective is to reduce citizen support for the system, provoke discontent and cause the targeted regime to fall from the inside.

In Nicaragua, LIC took three related forms. It began with support for insurgents, the contras; but, thanks to LIC, the contras were never classical guerrilla insurgents. The FSLN in its guerrilla days, the Frente Faribundo Marti para Liberacion Nacional (FMLN) in El Salvador, the Huks in the Philippines or the Viet Minh all had to scratch for their materiel, rely on the local population for food and intelligence, and have a sophisticated political message to win the people to their side. The contras, however, got their munitions, food, clothes and intelligence from the United States, so did not have to worry about political work: no matter how much they terrorized the population they would not be cut off from supplies. Unlike conventional insurgencies, the contras and other LIC guerrillas (e.g., Renamo in Mozambique) have greater license to engage in terrorism without suffering the consequences of lost political support.

I have argued that the Sandinistas waged a textbook counterinsurgency campaign against the contras, and would have defeated them well before the 1990 elections, but for the insurgents' extensive U.S. support.[12]

Had that happened, there would have been fewer deaths, less destruction, perhaps an end to conscription and certainly a start on reconstruction. Yet even had Washington abandoned its "pro-insurgency" policy, it still had plenty of options under LIC.

Economic pressure was applied through (1) eliminating Nicaragua's sugar quota; (2) imposing a full commercial embargo; (3) blocking loans to Nicaragua from international agencies; and (4) causing an estimated $12 billion in total damages to the Nicaraguan economy.[13] The United States also turned its diplomatic arsenal on the revolution. Especially important here were Washington's regional allies, who joined in the drive against the Sandinistas. Managua's friends in the developed world also felt the heat. In 1981, for example, France agreed to sell the Sandinistas $15.8 million in military equipment, but pressure from the Reagan administration caused the Mitterand government to cancel most of the deal.[14] Then in 1989 U.S. Secretary of State Baker convinced Nicaragua's European donors to defer a major meeting on aid until after the elections; this kept the FSLN from treating its economic woes before or during the campaign.

Military aggression that the government could contain but never eliminate, economic hardship and relentless external political pressure were all products of counterrevolutionary LIC. Their combined effect in Nicaragua was to limit the resources the Sandinistas had to meet its citizens' needs. LIC's impact was heightened by the Sandinistas' commitment to democracy. Since non-democratic governments ignore their citizens, LIC needs to spark a revolution or mount an invasion to work under those conditions. In countries that allow their citizens more freedom and which have more competitive politics, however, LIC has an advantage. People can vent their displeasure at the polls and bring in a new government. Open, democratic governments rely heavily on popular support. In a popular revolutionary regime, pledged to secure the "logic of the majority" this principle applies with special force.

We can go a step further. In an open regime, only the most obviously disloyal are excluded from politics. For example, in Nicaragua, only proponents of a return to Somocismo could not take office; but even they could express their views with some freedom, especially after the state of emergency was lifted in 1988. Thus, the most recalcitrant domestic foes of Sandinismo, the Coordinadora,[15] had political rights that made it an attractive target for U.S. funds; the same goes for the opposition media: *La Prensa,* Radio Catolica and Radio Corporacion. It is easy to see how the economic, psychological and military pressures that came with ten years of LIC set the stage for a Sandinista electoral defeat. But creating the conditions where losing became possible, even likely, could not ensure that the Sandinistas would actually lose. Certainly the FSLN campaigned expecting to win.

To understand how the UNO beat the FSLN on February 25th, 1990, we have to examine the details of the entire electoral process, not just the vote itself. This lets us judge if the FSLN might have won with different tactics. The Sandinista political project had given increasing importance to competitive politics and elections, and Washington's counterrevolutionary aggression was aimed at turning that growing pluralism against the FSLN. However, for the contras to pay their bills to the White House, Nicaraguans had to cast their ballots against the FSLN and for Washington's standard bearer.

Toward the 1990 Elections

To understand the 1990 elections in Nicaragua we must look at the 1984 contest.[16] That first taste of competitive politics came partly because the Sandinistas felt that winning fair, open elections would bring them enough international support to offset U.S.-backed attacks. But they also marked a watershed, dividing the radical past from a more conventional future. The FSLN was both serious and accurate when it said those elections were to institutionalize the revolution: 1985 brought new government institutions and the first steps toward a new and less radically transformational constitution. There are three things to remember about 1984's elections. First, they came before the economic collapse of the country; 1983 had even seen substantial growth. Second, though the war was real and menacing, it had not yet ground down people's resistance; thus patriotism would motivate people to vote for the revolutionary government. Finally, the opposition parties who actually ran — those furthest to the right boycotted the race in an effort to discredit the process — were very weak; they were in the race to establish their political credentials and thus ran against each other as much as against the FSLN. Added together with the Sandinistas' organizational skill and superior material resources, these factors spelled an easy win for president Daniel Ortega and the FSLN slate that captured 67 percent of the votes and 61 of 96 Assembly seats.

A fresh mandate in hand, the revolutionary government set about to secure peace and rein in an economy that was starting to spin out of control. Since they had to achieve both goals simultaneously and with limited resources, it was clear Nicaraguans were facing lean times. The impossibility of providing both guns and gallo pinto forced the state to impose three harsh austerity programmes between 1985 and 1989. These eliminated subsidies and jobs, but never effectively controlled the inflation that war always brings. All the while, the war itself dragged on.

Although the military declared the "strategic defeat" of the contras in 1986 (meaning that the insurgents were permanently on the defensive and no longer threatened the state itself), U.S. assistance to the guerrillas ensured that they would not be totally defeated. While the contras remained active, they had to be fought. To fight them, the Sandinista Army needed conscripts; and conscripts meant that families throughout the country would not forget the war or their government's inability to end it.

If peace eluded the Sandinistas' grasp, it was not for lack of effort. Even before the 1984 elections the revolutionary state had repeatedly sought a negotiated end to the conflict. In retrospect, it seems those efforts were doomed because the Sandinistas confronted the might of the United States with no support from their neighbours. Things began to change after the second Esquipulas conference (August 1987) when all five Central American presidents signed a peace accord without Washington's approval.[17]

Esquipulas II (better known in North America as the Arias Plan, after the Costa Rican president who was its principal architect) aimed to bring peace to the entire region. Its intent was to cover all countries confronting protracted conflicts. That only Nicaragua and Costa Rica — which faced neither insurgency nor violent domestic unrest — complied with the treaty's provisions is a telling comment on the other states' political will.

To meet its obligations, the FSLN government dropped all restrictions on its political opposition within six months. Within nine months, the Sandinistas had gone beyond the treaty's demands and started talks with the counterrevolutionaries. In return, the Sandinistas expected that no country in the region would let its territory be used to attack Nicaragua and that *all* aid to the contras would cease. In short, the revolutionary government traded domestic political concessions for an end to the fighting. The Sandinistas kept their side of the bargain. The others, led by the U.S. government, did not.

On October 5th, 1987, again complying with the Esquipulas treaty, the Nicaraguan government initiated a National Dialogue with eight opposition parties, which later expanded to fifteen political organizations, including the Coordinadora. From the start, the meetings were fractious. Squabbling within the opposition was common, and parties withdrew from and returned to the sessions like yo-yos. Yet it was this assemblage, representing the traditional right, the modernizing centre and the orthodox Marxist-Leninist left, that laid the foundations for today's UNO government.

At the Dialogue's eleventh meeting, November 26th, 1987, the opposition presented a list of seventeen constitutional amendments, making its participation in the talks conditional on the immediate enactment of the proposed reforms. "Christians believe that God created the world in seven days, so I don't see why the government can't agree to these changes in the same amount of time," quipped Liberal Orlando Quinonez.[18] The Sandinistas rejected the package, arguing that meeting the demands of "the Bloc of 14," a "historical convergence" of fourteen parties of all ideological stripes, would have violated the 1987 Constitution (which six of the Fourteen voted to approve a year earlier). The opposition then walked out for good.

A year later some of the Fourteen concluded that the seventeen demands had been a mistake.[19] More moderate segments of the Bloc felt that they had lost the strength they had built since 1984 and handed back leadership of the opposition to the Coordinadora, the U.S. embassy's favourites. These moderates, drawn from several different parties, had different strategies for regaining their momentum. Some of the centrists wanted sub-alliances, for example, a Democratic Centre Bloc of six. Others, further to the right, looked to Alfredo Cesar, recently returned from self-imposed exile in Costa Rica, to take charge. A third group pinned its hopes on Independent Liberal Caudillo Virgilio Godoy. At the end of 1988, a unified opposition was nowhere in sight. With the opposition in seemingly terminal disarray, the FSLN kept searching for peace. In February 1989 it signed the Esquipulas IV accords in El Salvador. The five

Central American heads of state approved a Nicaraguan proposal to move the contras from Honduras and assist their resettlement in either Nicaragua or a third country. For its part, the FSLN agreed to: 1) change the election date from the constitutionally-fixed November 1990 to 25 February 1990; 2) release prisoners, including ex-Somoza National Guards, on a case-by-case basis; 3) give equal television and radio access to both the government and opposition parties; and 4) invite international observers, including the United Nations and Organization of American States, to monitor the entire electoral process.[20]

Once again the Sandinistas traded domestic political room for peace; and once again it did not work. Disregarding the will of the Central American leaders, Congress gave the contras $66 million to sustain them through the elections, after which Washington would have another look. Nevertheless, the Sandinistas pressed ahead with their electoral plans. They really had no other choice: walking away from their Esquipulas IV commitments would have given the United States the perfect excuse to send massive military aid to the counterrevolutionaries.

Despite these setbacks, the Sandinistas continued accommodating the opposition, doing all they could to avoid a repetition of 1984's boycott by the Coordinadora and last minute withdrawal by Godoy's Liberals. Without an opposition slate that included the preferred choice of the U.S. embassy, Managua knew that George Bush would resurrect Ronald Reagan's "Soviet sham elections" speech and let the war grind on. So, to deny their foes a pretext for not running, the Sandinistas amended two laws. One eliminated a five per cent threshold for representation in the National Assembly; the other allowed unlimited foreign contributions to any political party, provided that half the funds go to the electoral office (CSE or Supreme Electoral Council) to cover general expenses. Both satisfied, at least momentarily, opposition demands.

Persistence appeared to pay off for the Sandinistas six months before the elections. The UNO made its first official appearance on the national scene and surprised observers by agreeing to a formula for elections. Their participation did not come cheaply: suspending the military draft from 1 September 1989 through election day was only one of the concessions the FSLN had to make.[21] Still, this seemed a good deal, because it gave Daniel Ortega all-party backing for his electoral plans as he set off for still another peace conference. This one, at Tela, Honduras, approved another scheme for demobilizing and repatriating the contras, under United Nations supervision, by December 1989. This would be just in time for the formal start of the election campaign.

Why did the Sandinistas keep going back to the poisoned well? Two years of trading internal political space for peace gave opponents of both the government and the revolution lots of operating room, but peace still only came from successful military operations. One explanation is that failing to grant political concessions would let U.S. hawks give the contras even more money and weapons. There is, though, another possibility.

A series of polls done between June 1988 and September 1989 tended to show the Sandinistas in the lead.[22] I say "tended," because the results from the surveys were mixed. For example, one done by the Costa Rican pollster, Victor Borge, gave the opposition a 49-25 edge over the government; yet one carried out a bit later by Marvin Ortega's Managua think-tank, Itztani, showed the FSLN winning 37-16. Now Borge was hired by *La Prensa* and Ortega was identified with the government,[23] so one might view these results sceptically. But a survey done coincidentally with Ortega's by the independent Manolo Morales Foundation and published by the weekly *La Cronica* (linked to the Popular Social Christian Party), matched Itztani's findings. These data were enough to give the Sandinistas the confidence to keep following their chosen path.

The Campaign and Its Outcome

The growing pluralism of the Sandinista state made competitive elections in 1990 plausible and possible. The continued military and economic pressure applied by the counterrevolutionary policies of the United States made the 1990 elections the most important in Nicaragua's history. Voters were going to pass judgement on the FSLN's capacity as a builder and manager. They would have to decide if, despite the horrors and hardships of the contras' war, continuing the Sandinista revolution remained the best hope for their country. All ten campaigns (the FSLN, the UNO and eight minor parties)[24] had different answers to that question.

If this had been an "ins versus outs" election, as in neighbouring Honduras and Costa Rica, the Sandinistas would never have had a chance. Five years of economic chaos would have routed any conventional party from office. It was only because the Sandinistas had something to offer Nicaraguans besides their record that they could even dream of winning. Defending, promoting and expanding the goals and values of 1979 distinguished the FSLN from its opponents.

Curiously, though, this theme was not given a high profile in the 1989-1990 race.[25] Rather, the Sandinistas focused their energies on making Daniel Ortega a star. Daniel shed his glasses, donned tight jeans and bright shirts and became the "gallo ennavajado" — the gamecock with steel spurs — fit to be president of "this fighting people," as a campaign song put it. The Sandinistas' main theme was: "With Daniel and (his running mate) Sergio (Ramirez) everything will be better!"

Believing that a personality-based campaign would capture the most votes, the FSLN extended this down to the local level. Nicaragua was awash with t-shirts bearing the name and likeness of myriad Sandinista candidates. Billboards and walls were plastered or painted with the "Todo sera mejor" ("Everything will be better") slogan, prefaced by "Con/With (the local candidate)." But it was at party rallies that the stars shone.

Sandinista rallies were works of Central American political art. The president, often with his vice-president, would arrive in town at the head of a troop of 100 or more horsemen, or marching down the main street or riding in what people called the "Danielmobile." This was a mobile platform carrying Ortega, Ramirez and a cluster of local candidates. As the Danielmobile passed people would thrust their children up into the waiting hands of the candidates and advisors, who passed them to Ortega. Then Polaroids snapped and the child was returned clutching a snapshot of herself or himself in the president's arms. Once at the plaza or the ballfield where the show was scheduled, Ortega would mount the stage that, along with a mammoth sound system, travelled with him, and begin his routine. The theatrical metaphor is appropriate, because these rallies were as carefully scripted and choreographed as any Broadway hit. Music was provided by groups playing campaign songs made familiar by all the air time they got on the state and party radio stations, the most powerful in Nicaragua. Daniel would lead cheers, throw out baseballs to the crowd and give a tub-thumping political speech.

Actually, Daniel gave *the* speech. There was, of course, some tailoring done for the local audience, but after two or three rallies you really did know the drill. Ortega introduced himself as both the incumbent and the president-elect, and then proceeded to declare all the local hopefuls elected, too. He would then berate the UNO for its ties to the counterrevolution, peppering his speeches with reference to the "GN-UNO," the "(Somoza) National Guard-UNO." This let him make the point that the FSLN was the party of peace, while the UNO, with ties to the contras and Somocismo, was the war party.

Impressive as the rallies were, and they were impressive partly because the Sandinistas trucked lots of people to them,[26] the FSLN electoral machine did not stop there. Around 50,000 activists were formed into electoral action committees who put up posters and carried out thorough canvasses.[27] These canvasses, backed up by public and internal polls, convinced the Sandinistas the election was in the bag. Even where they were weakest, the departments of Boaco and Chontales (Region V), party officials predicted a saw-off between the FSLN and the UNO. And in the town of Teustepe, which returned the largest opposition vote in 1984, the local Sandinista organizer declared: "You might not believe this, but we've got 62.5% of the voters in this municipality voting for us."[28]

In contrast to the slick, almost gaudy, Sandinista campaign the UNO's efforts appeared amateurish and underfunded.[29] Part of their problem was inexperienced candidates and organizers. Their presidential candidate, Violeta Chamorro, had no previous campaign background and owed her nomination to having been a natural compromise candidate in a hung convention. Though Dona Violeta brought the magical Chamorro name to the campaign (she is the widow of Pedro Joaquin Chamorro, the publisher of *La Prensa* assassinated by Somoza thugs in 1978) and possessed a warm, grandmotherly demeanour, her early appearances on the stump were disasters: reading a speech from note cards and fluffing the lines is not most Nicaraguans' idea of a leader.

The parties (See Table 1) were in no better shape. Of the fourteen who formed the UNO, only four — the Socialists, Communists, Independent Liberals and the Popular Social Christians[30] — had any electoral experience. Many were tiny and without any real organization; and since the fourteen ranged from the orthodox Marxism-Leninism of the Communists to the orthodox Somocismo of the Authentic Liberals, they were united only by their desire to beat the Frente.

TABLE 1

The UNO Coalition

National Conservative Party	Independent Liberal Party
Conservative Popular Alliance	Authentic Liberal Party
Conservative National Action Party	Liberal Constitutionalist Party
Democratic Party of National Confidence	National Action Party
Central American Integrationist Party	Social Democratic Party
Nicaraguan Socialist Party	Popular Social Christian Party
Communist Party of Nicaragua	Nicaraguan Democratic Movement

Moreover, their campaign was riddled with accidents. The presidential candidate broke her knee and was out of action for over a month. Her running-mate, Virgilio Godoy, was alleged to have embezzled funds from his Independent Liberal Party.[31] Godoy also fell out with other UNO chieftains, for example barring campaign manager Antonio Lacayo and top Chamorro advisor and Assembly candidate Alfredo Cesar from the platform when he spoke.[32] More serious, though out of the public eye, the Campaign Committee of the UNO, made up of Mrs. Chamorro's backers, constantly battled the party's Political Council, where Mr. Godoy's supporters dominated. Rumour had it that the coalition almost blew apart in January 1990 when some leaders tried unsuccessfully to secure a formal denunciation of the contras.

Though the UNO campaign came together in the last two weeks of the race, it looked like too little, too late. Still, the UNO had its strengths, among them a clear, simple message: 'Turn the Sandinistas out and bring us in. Then you will have peace and prosperity'. This appealed to a large audience who felt it was time for a change. Its promise to end conscription appealed to draft age boys and their parents. President Bush's commitment to lift the U.S. embargo if the UNO won sounded good to small businesspeople. Still, the UNO's platform was just a conventional right-of-centre plan to strengthen the market and the bourgeoisie and offered the average Nicaraguan very little. Seen from the Nicaraguan ground on the eve of the vote, the Sandinistas' organization appeared ready and able to pull the election out of the fire.[33] But when the smoke cleared, we found that UNO had won the election (see Table 2).

TABLE 2

1990 Nicaraguan Election Results

Party	Percentage of Vote	Assembly Seats
UNO	54.7	51
FSLN	40.8	39*
Others	5.52**	
Turnout	86.2	

(Source: CSE, *Boletines Informativos*, March 1-3, 1990)

*The FSLN won an extra Assembly seat because its presidential candidate won 1/90 of the national vote.
**One seat was won by the United Revolutionary Movement, whose presidential candidate passed the 1/90 threshold; the other went to the Social Christian Alliance, but is held by Yatama, the Miskitu party, which provided the Social Christian slate where the seat was won.

What Could Have Been Done?

What happened? First, the Sandinistas' political intelligence failed them completely. The companero in Teustepe who said five-eighths of his neighbours supported the FSLN missed badly: 80.6 percent of the Teustepenos voted UNO.[34] The reasons for this massive breakdown that kept the Sandinistas from adjusting their campaign were recognized by the Frente in a June 1990 congress. "Verticalism," the top-down structure shared by all vanguard parties, was the principal culprit. It separated the leaders from the base.

Better information from the bases would have told the Sandinistas that the lavishness of their rallies offended people. It would have let them know that their triumphalism was sending people to vote for the UNO to cut the FSLN's victory margin. They would have discovered that the GN-UNO theme troubled voters, reminding them of the early 1980s when Sandinista activists could accuse citizens of being Somocistas or contras with impunity. Finally, they would have found that their policies sat badly with the popular classes. Walking back from the UNO's closing rally amidst hundreds of Dona Violeta's supporters, I heard a mildly drunken man cry out as we passed the Casa de Gobierno (the main government office building): "The Sandinistas give cars and trucks to cotton growers. They give money and tax breaks to other big producers. They are always giving something to the rich. But what do they give us, the poor? Not a goddamn thing!"

One thing the Sandinistas might have done was stop the military draft. During the last two weeks of the campaign rumours flew that a surprise was coming. Everyone figured it had to be the continued suspension, if not elimination, of conscription, because the Sandinista leadership had specifically denied the draft was involved. The big announcement was supposed to have been made at the FSLN's closing rally, February 21st, but nothing happened. Later, sources close to the Sandinista campaign said Ortega originally intended to end conscription, but changed his mind when he saw a crowd of 250,000 in the plaza before him.[35]

We cannot know if anything would have brought the Sandinistas the 100,000 votes they needed to win. However, we can speculate about what would have happened if the FSLN had won. Though the dominant, moderate wing of the UNO was gracious in victory, and while Cardinal Obando was calling on all sides to accept the voters' verdict weeks before the election, some in the UNO held a different view.

Throughout the campaign the UNO's officials, supporters and foreign advisors spoke of "environmental fraud." They meant that the advantages enjoyed by the Sandinistas as incumbents were so great that even an election pronounced technically honest by UN and OAS observers would still have been essentially rigged. In particular, they stressed the government's control of television and the country's two largest radio stations, its access to state-owned trucks and buses and its freedom to use the security forces to harass and intimidate the opposition.[36]

When reminded that incumbency had its costs as well, they talked about fraudulent vote counting. Alfredo Cesar announced that the UNO would have people protesting in the streets if the official results released by the CSE did not match their samples.[37] Even more provocative was Virgilio Godoy's interview with the Spanish daily, *Diario 16*, where he claimed "the Sandinistas can win, for example, if they have Violeta

Chamorro assassinated, if they have me assassinated, if they decapitate the UNO, maybe they could win."[38] Yet the fact that the contras were kidnapping and killing Sandinista activists and threatening to kill anyone voting for the FSLN[39] was dismissed by saying that the contras did not work for the UNO.[40]

This suggests that a Sandinista win would have brought howls of protest from parts of the UNO. Presumably those protests would have got a friendly hearing in the White House, although Congress might have been harder to convince had the international observers issued a clean bill of health. But none of this matters because Nicaraguans decided that re-electing the FSLN would not bring peace, while electing the UNO would.

The day after the elections, while the vote was still being counted, the pro-Sandinista *El Nuevo Diario* carried the headline, "Bush is winning." In a sense he and imperialist interests everywhere did win, because the Sandinistas lost office. Yet it overstates the case to say that U.S. imperialism was totally responsible for the revolutionary government's electoral defeat. There were things the FSLN could have done to salvage the vote, but they were terribly overconfident and badly misread the electorate. And re-elected FSLN would have kept power, but it would have had to keep fighting the contras and every other form of LIC Washington could devise.

So LIC did contribute to the Sandinistas' loss in two ways. First, it created conditions that made the FSLN government unpopular. This proved important because the Sandinistas had come to emphasize elections. Opening the revolutionary political process combined with the effects of LIC (war and economic devastation) to produce a second consequence: narrowing of the political space in which the government could work. Thus, the contra war and its associated economic havoc created an electoral conjuncture where the Sandinistas could win only by running a superb campaign.

Conclusion

The 1990 elections showed the Sandinistas the importance of keeping in touch with their supporters. The problem, of course, is that pro-insurgent LIC makes governments shuffle their priorities, putting fence mending and constituency relations well below defence. It might seem odd that this happened to the Sandinistas, one of the most responsive political forces in Latin America. Yet despite their commitment to democracy and opening the system to the marginalized, the Sandinistas' internal organization remained a rigid, top-down, democratic centralism. "Verticalism" is indispensable to a revolutionary vanguard and useful to any government in time of emergency, but it closed the FSLN off from its supporters, who then turned it out of office.

A party congress held in June 1990, set the FSLN down a new path. Self-criticism produced the admission that the party hierarchy had lost touch with the rank-and-file and come to prefer giving orders to discussing issues. As well, an ethics commission was struck to investigate charges of corruption and abuse of power. Finally, the Frente recognized that it was off centre-stage and had to prepare the party to fight and win elections in 1996.[41]

No sooner had the congress ended than the Sandinistas confronted a new challenge. A wave of strikes, led by Sandinista unions, challenged the Chamorro government and showed the FSLN that Nicaragua now boasted powerful popular movements that did not need its leadership. The one-time vanguard must now learn to channel and coordinate spontaneous demands from those opposing the UNO regime to regain power.[42]

Putting the FSLN in opposition and substantially deradicalizing it did not, however, satisfy Washington. Nor did the Chamorro administration meet U.S. expectations, because it did not destroy the Sandinistas. Thus, the U.S. embassy in Managua made clear its support for vice-president Virgilio Godoy, leader of the hard-line, anti-Sandinista faction. Washington upped the ante in late 1990 with a U.S. Agency for International Development grant to a group of UNO mayors who wanted Godoy to replace Chamorro as Nicaragua's president and get on with the business of wiping out all traces of Sandinista influence. U.S. imperialists plainly do not think they won in Nicaragua, so Bush's "new world order" must be secured.

In Nicaragua, U.S. policy demands the disappearance of the FSLN. For the Frente to thwart Washington's aims and remain a political option, it must become an efficient electoral party while retaining its transformational zeal. Further, the UNO government must become sufficiently pluralistic and democratic to let the FSLN function as an opposition and the government-in-waiting. Above all, the Sandinistas must defend the vital accomplishments of the revolution (e.g., land reform) to solidify their electoral base for 1996. In short, they have to learn to combine electoral-parliamentary struggle with movement-based politics. If this happens, the FSLN can hand the contras and their imperialist sponsors a final defeat when they return to office. And hopefully the regional political climate will be more supportive of popular social transformation on Nicaragua (see Broad, Chapter Seven).

Notes

1. Hemisphere Initiative, *Nicaraguan Election Update #2: Foreign Funding for the Internal Opposition*. Boston, MA, 1989.
2. Those wanting more background on Sandinista Nicaragua should consult the following books, all in English: George Black, *The Triumph of the People*. London: Zed Books, 1982; John Booth, *The End and the Beginning*. Boulder: Westview, 1985; David Close, *Nicaragua: Politics, Economics and Society*. London: Frances Pinter, 1988; Jose Corragio, *Nicaragua: Revolution and Democracy*. Winchester, MA: Allen and Unwin, 1985; Dennis Gilbert, *Sandinistas*. Oxford: Basil Blackwell, 1988; Richard Harris, and Carlos Vilas, *Nicaragua: A Revolution Under Seige*. London: Zed Books, 1985; Kent Norsworthy, *Nicaragua: A Country Guide*. Albuquerque, NM: The Resource Centre, 1989; Rose Spalding, *The Political Economy of Revolutionary Nicaragua*. Winchester, MA: Allen and Unwin, 1987; Carlos Vilas. *The Sandinista Revolution*. New York: Monthly Review Press, 1987; and *State, Class and Ethnicity in Nicaragua*. Boulder: Lynne Reiner, 1989; Thomas Walker, *Nicaragua in Revolution*. New York: Praeger, 1982; and *Nicaragua: The First Five Years*. New York: Praeger, 1985.
3. Steven Gorman, "Power and consolidation in the Nicaraguan revolution," *Journal of Latin American Studies*, Vol.13: No. 1, May, 1981, pp. 133-149.
4. Good evidence of the social pluralism of Sandinismo was the policy, in place until 1984, of giving privileged access to hard currency to those who needed it to pay the tuition for the children in foreign schools.
5. Gary Rurchwarger, *People in Power*. South Hadley, MA: Bergin and Garvey, 1987.
6. The Council of State was composed of members appointed by organizations; e.g., the Sandinista Army, Sandinsta Defence Committees, the Sandinista Youth, political parties, unions and business associations. The National Assembly has elected members sitting for geographical constituencies.
7. Like any civic pact that enables government to function normally in a state marked by dramatic social cleavages, this one set limits on all political actors. The following quote from Comandante Jaime Wheelock, one of the nine Comandantes de la Revolucion who formed the National Directorate of the FSLN, gives a sense how far tolerance extended.

"(The opposition) can be anti-Sandinistas, they can be against the Frente Sandinista as a political party, they can criticize us, but they cannot attack the bases of the new society that are in the historical interest of the people of Nicaragua....These people can even be non-revolutionary, but they cannot be counterrevolutionary" (quoted in David Close, *Nicaragua: Politics, Economics and Society.* London: Frances Pinter, 1988).

8. Max Azicri, "Comparing two social revolutions: the dynamics of change in Cuba and Nicaragua," *Communist Studies,* Vol. 5: No. 4, Dec. 1989, pp. 17-39.
9. We should distinguish between anti-revolutionaries, who would dismantle a revolution's policies if they took power but who stay within the law, from counterrevolutionaries who will break the law to end the revolution. In Nicaragua, the two often cooperated, but not always.
10. John Saul, "Destabilization in Mozambique," *Studies in Political Economy,* No. 23, May, 1987, pp. 5-40.
11. Waghelstein, J., "Post-Vietnam counterinsurgency doctrine," *Military Review,* Vol. 65: No. 5, 1985.
12. David Close, "Counterinsurgency in Nicaragua," *New Political Science,* No. 18/19 (Fall/Winter 1990).
13. Note, though, Helwege's argument that economic instruments had to be of secondary importance because "the USA did not have much leverage over the Sandinistas through economic sanctions." Helwege, A., "Three socialist experiences in Latin America: surviving U.S. economic pressure," *Bulletin of Latin American Research,* Vol. 8: No. 2, 1989.
14. Matthews, R., "The limits of friendship: Nicaragua and the west," *NACLA Report on the America,* Vol. 19: No. 3, 1985.
15. The Nicaraguan Democratic Coordinator, or Coordinadora, represented the most radically anti-Sandinista elements in Nicaragua who did not take up arms against the government. Its most important constituent was COSEP, the Superior Council of Private Enterprise, the apex group of Nicaragua's big business organizations. Several small political parties, the AFL-linked union and part of the Christian Democratic union also belonged.
16. David Close, "The Nicaraguan Elections of 1984," *Electoral Studies,* Vol. 5: No. 2, 1985; Lasa, "Report of the Latin American Studies Association delegation to observe the Nicaraguan General Elections of November 4, 1984," *LASA Forum,* Vol. 15: No. 4, 1985
17. Editors' Note: Esquipulas is the town in Guatemala where the five Central American presidents met in 1987 to sign a program for regional peace that was worked out by Costa Rican President Oscar Arias. The treaty called on combatants in El Salvador and Nicaragua to commit themselves to a cease-fire; called on the United States to cease funding the contras; and called on the Sandinistas to hold elections. The plan won President Arias a Nobel Peace Prize.
18. *Update,* December 20, 1987: p. 3, Central American Historical Institute, Washington, D.C.
19. Material in this section comes from interviews with representatives of the Fourteen conducted in Nicaragua during October and November 1988.
20. CAR, *Central America Report,* February 17, 1989, Guatemala City, Guatemala.
21. *Envio,* September 1989, Washington, D.C. and Managua, Nicaragua.
22. *Envio,* February 1990: pp. 13-16, Washington, D.C. and Managua, Nicaragua.
23. Marvin Ortega is not related to Daniel and Humberto Ortega, and has never been a member of the FSLN, although his political sympathies lie with the revolution.

24. The eight minor parties were: 1) the Left — United Revolutionary Movement; Revolutionary Workers Party; Popular Action Movement — ML; 2) the Centre — Central American Unionist Party; Independent Liberal Party of National Unity; Social Christian Alliance; Conservative Democratic Party; 3) the Right — Social Conservative Party. Half of the Social Christian Alliance (the Popular Social Christian Party), the Popular Action Movement — ML, and the Conservative Democratic Party had run in 1984 and held seats in the National Assembly.
25. Most of the information contained in this section was collected in Nicaragua from January through March 1990, and is based on personal observation, including many informal conversations. Specific citations are included where appropriate.
26. Trucking people to election rallies is a Central American tradition, honed to its finest edge in Costa Rica, where they have the most experience with elections. Those unfamiliar with the region's political mores frown upon this practice, but it is not a bad indicator of a party's resources and organizational or mobilizational capacity. To the extent that money and the ability to muster people on cue are useful in politics, these rallies say something about a party's strength.
27. *Barricada*, February 12, 90: p. 13, Managua, Nicaragua.
28. Author's Personal Interview, 90.02.15
29. How this could happen to a "civic opposition" that had received an estimated $29 million since 1985 (Hemisphere Initiatives, *Nicaraguan Election Update #2: Foreign Funding for the Internal Opposition*. Boston, MA, 1989) is perplexing. Perhaps the stories of new cars and houses for UNO party leaders had some substance. More to the point, the UNO was so bereft of volunteers and organization that they paid for everything and everybody, even poll watchers; thus even a lot of money would not have gone far. When I told an organizer for the conservative Costa Rican Social Christian Unity Party how the UNO spent its money, he could only bless himself and sigh.
30. The Popular Social Christians were originally part of the UNO, but one wing, led by Mauricio Diaz, split and joined Erik Ramirez of the Social Christians to run as a third party. By their own account, those who stayed in the UNO did so because they felt they would win more seats.
31. CAR, *Central America Report*, December 8, 1989: 384, Guatemala City, Guatemala.
32. *Barricada Internacional*, January 20, 1990: p. 9, Managua, Nicaragua.
33. Reliable sources reported that, when paid an election-eve courtesy call by the Soviet ambassador, Mrs. Chamorro assured her visitor that the UNO had only been in this race to gain experience and fully expected to lose.
34. Consejo Supremo Electoral (CSE), *Boletines Informativos*, March 2, 1990, Managua, Nicaragua.
35. The massive turnout for the closing of the campaign, easily five times larger than the UNO's closing rally, raises a key point. Throughout the campaign the Sandinistas showed repeatedly that they could mobilize people. On election night, the results proved that getting voters to go to your rallies is not the same thing as persuading them to vote for you.
36. *International Herald Tribune*, January 26, 1990, Paris and New York; *La Nacion*, January 26, 1990, San Jose, Costa Rica.
37. *Barricada*, February 15, 1990, Managua, Nicaragua.
38. *Barricada*, February 14, 1990: p. 4, Managua, Nicaragua.
39. *Nicaragua Through Our Eyes*, March-April, 1990: p. 2, Managua, Nicaragua.
40. Personal interview with member of UNO, 90.02.16.
41. This liberalization began soon after the elections; and can be traced back as far as a 1989 interview with Sergio Ramirez (La Cronica, 89.12.15). (Brannigan, W., "Sandinistas weigh shift to mainstream," *Washington Post*, 15 April, 1990).

42. This may give the more confrontational wing of the party, home to the strongest Leninist elements, a chance to assert its claims to leadership. As a result, reforming the FSLN's organization and defining a new image for the Frente might be more difficult than first thought.

Chapter Six

The Privatization of War: Low Intensity Imperialism in the Philippines

Douglas W. Booker

In February 1986, a "people's revolt" in support of a failed coup attempt swept the corrupt regime of Ferdinand Marcos from power and installed Corazon Aquino as president of the Philippines. Within the Philippines, this change was welcomed in political circles from the centre to the national democratic left. The change was also welcomed by the international community, and in particular the United States, to whom these events afforded the opportunity of dumping one of its empire's more tarnished political figures. The American's eagerness to unseat Marcos was evident in the central role they played in brokering his departure and eventually flying him out of the country and resettling him in Hawaii.[1]

The new president, Corazon Aquino, projected a more moderate image, representative of the new order America was constructing among its satellites in the 1980s (e.g., South Korea, El Salvador, and now, Panama). In the Philippines, it was widely believed this new order would open up a democratic space for much broader participation, particularly for the left, who had been driven underground during the Marcos regime.[2] It was hoped that President Aquino's platform of national reconciliation and her strong support for human rights, combined with her immense popularity, would translate into greater control over an abusive military and provide her with the power to launch much needed social and economic reforms.

Initially, a Presidential Commission on Human Rights (PCHR) was established to investigate the "alleged" abuses of the military, followed later by peace talks with the NDF[3] aimed at national reconciliation. In the aftermath, however, of both numerous coup attempts and sabotaged peace negotiations with the National Democratic Front (NDF), Aquino's program of reconciliation was abandoned. The President subsequently went on record as saying that the answer to the insurgency was "not social and economic reform, but police and military action."[4] The President's militant statement was backed up by a more active counterinsurgency program, evident in the peasant massacre at Lupao, in increased aerial bombing campaigns, and in the growing numbers of refugees from areas of military operations.

The most salient feature of the Aquino government's counterinsurgency program has been the emergence and proliferation of paramilitary vigilante groups. As of July 1987, the Philippine Alliance for Human Rights Advocates (PAHRA) reported the emergence of some 77 vigilante groups throughout the Philippines; 27 in Luzon, 31 in the Visayas, and 13 in Mindanao.[5] The proliferation of these vigilante squads has been described by the government and military as a spontaneous uprising against the abuses of the New People's Army (NPA).[6] According to President Aquino, these militant anti-communist groups are a "genuine grassroots expression of people's power." It is interesting to note, however, that the rise of the death squads has paralleled a new commitment of official covert U.S. aid through the CIA and increased "private aid" through channels of the American New Right.

The post-Marcos Philippines reflects two developing tendencies in U.S. foreign policy. The first is what Suzanne Jonas has called the double game, in which U.S. policymakers claim to be building the "moderate centre" (which in the case of Central America has been necessary to insure funding from Congress) while at the same time building the extreme right.[7] The second element is what can be termed the privatization of U.S. foreign policy. A policy first witnessed in action when the U.S. Congress halted aid to the contras forcing Oliver North to raise funds elsewhere. In the Philippines, the vigilantes can be viewed as one element in a comprehensive strategy aimed at privatizing the war against the insurgents.

This campaign has drawn on the resources, ideological convictions, and the power of the "private sector" both within the Philippines and at an international level to facilitate and complement state initiatives and objectives.

The phenomenon of private aid has increasingly become an important element of U.S. foreign policy in the 1980s, as the United States moved in the direction of a global rollback strategy under Reagan (see Chapter Two above). The re-emergence of the global rollback strategy, premised on the idea of pushing back and wiping out communism, can be attributed to the victory of the Sandinistas in Nicaragua and the growth of the New Right in the United States. While this never became official U.S. government policy, the Reagan administration allowed proponents of this strategy to operate within the White House and utilize its resources to pursue the strategy. The strategy remained, however, dependent on private assistance to be operationalized.

The Iran-Contra events demonstrated just how significant the private networks have become as an instrument of American foreign policy. While in the Philippines the private sources have not been used to circumvent the directives of the U.S. Congress, as was the case with the Nicaraguan contras, these sources have been central to establishing a new version of the "freedom fighter," known as the vigilante in the former American colony. It will be argued here that the rise of paramilitary forces in the Philippines is part of a government-orchestrated campaign of counterinsurgency premised on the U.S. Low Intensity Conflict (LIC) strategy, and most significantly, fundamentally supported by "private" sources from within the United States.

The chapter will first examine the application of this strategy in the Philippines, focusing on the central role played by non-government agencies and personalities in both the ideological and military application of termed Low Intensity Conflict. The analysis will focus on both the involvement of foreign nationals and foreign organizations in anti-communist ideological work within the Philippines, and on the apparent subcontracting of military and propaganda operations to vigilante squads and religious cults. After looking at LIC strategy this chapter then examines the impact on both the legal and revolutionary left, and the response of these groups to Low Intensity Conflict.

Low Intensity Conflict

One of the notable features of the vigilantes is the seemingly odd combination of paramilitary squads and fundamentalist religious cults in the growing privatization of the war against "communism." This union is not indigenous to the Philippines, having been utilized in various U.S. client states, including South Vietnam, El Salvador, and Guatemala. The program of vigilante terrorism is a component of a new U.S. strategy, developed primarily from experiences in Vietnam, which is aimed at defeating or containing national liberation movements which might be regarded as threats to U.S. strategic and commercial interests. This approach has been termed "Low Intensity Conflict" in Pentagon warfare manuals. The term "low intensity" misleadingly suggests a small scale conventional war, obscuring the fact that for those countries involved the intensity is anything but low.

What distinguishes LIC from regular warfare is the character of the conflict. According to Dr. Sam Sarkesian,

> LIC evolves primarily from revolutionary and counterinsurgency strategy and causes, and therefore, includes unconventional operations, protractedness, and high political and psychological content directly linked to the political-social milieu of the indigenous area.[8]

LIC was designed to instigate war at the grassroots level among civilians and rebels through the organization of civilian agents of the military in both open armed confrontation and psychological warfare. LIC concentrates both its propaganda and military efforts on the non-combatant, non-militant population in order to confuse, sow doubt, divide and neutralize their support for the insurgency.

In this application of LIC, the Philippine government has turned to vigilantes in order to sow terror and create conditions which make it impossible for insurgents to organize in the affected areas. Since LIC strategists believe that the continued existence of the NPA depends on a supportive population, LIC aims to isolate the revolutionary movement from the masses by taking the war to the grassroots level. This means that the war will not only be waged against the armed rebels in isolated areas but will also be fought in the communities, taking the form of civilian vigilante groups and the general militarization of populated areas. This strategy effectively privatizes and localizes the war against the insurgents.

Privatizing the Terror

Vigilantism embodies the LIC concept of using surrogate forces in covert military operations. Civilians, including children, are being organised into extra-judicial units of military commands and operations in the name of preserving democracy and freedom. The utilization of cults and vigilante groups has four main advantages. First, it allows the government to reduce expenses because all these groups need are firearms and immunity. Second, it improves intelligence operations because these groups emerge out of local communities. Third, the vigilante groups assist the military with its public relations problems because they do the "messy part of the job" for the military[9] (i.e., arbitrary arrest and "salvaging"[10]). Finally, for the Americans, it maximizes the use of indigenous forces in counterrevolutionary warfare, allowing them to avoid any commitment of ground troops in these local struggles to "rollback" communism.

In many ways, these vigilantes are an extension of programs overtly and covertly organized under the previous regime. In Mindanao, fanatical sects were utilized by the military against Muslims in the late 1960s and early 1970s, and later against suspected sympathizers of the NPA. Under Marcos many of these cults, such as the *Ilaga* (Rats), Rock Christ, 4Ks and the infamous *Tadtad* (chop chop), were brought into the Integrated Civilian Home Defence Force (ICHDF). They assisted the military in counterinsurgency operations, terrorized rural farmers, and carried out mass killings in remote barrios and mountain regions. The major differences between the contemporary vigilante and those armed under the Marcos regime was that Marcos denied any support for or connection to these organizations, whereas today's vigilantes enjoy both the financial and moral support of the Aquino regime.

Since the collapse of ceasefire talks in February 1987, the Aquino government has provided open support for both fanatical and vigilante groups as an element of the "total war" program against the insurgency. On April 6, 1987, the government issued guidelines for the "legalization" of vigilante groups.[11] Just over one month later, Secretary of Local Government, Jaime Ferrer,[12] barnstormed the country ordering governors and mayors to establish vigilante groups. In Mindanao, he gave fifteen appointed governors two months to organize vigilante groups or be fired.

By November 1987, the government adopted a set of guidelines which legitimized the military functions of the groups and authorized the military to take responsibility for their training, supervision, and coordination. These guidelines also permitted the arming of the vigilantes.[13] Currently, with the expressed authorization of President Aquino, right-wing vigilante groups have been formed throughout the Philippines, including Alsa Masa in Davao City, the Nakasaka in Davao del Sur, the Citizens-Against Communism Army (CACA), and KADRE in Cebu province.[14] In many areas existing religious cults and vigilante groups such as the 4K in South Cotabato and the Tadtad in Cebu, Davao del Sur and Davao City have simply been integrated into the government's "official" vigilante groups.

The prototype of the post-ceasefire vigilante group is *Alsa Masa* (mass uprising) of Davao City. Where Davao City was earlier a testing ground for the NPA's urban guerilla warfare, it has now become the experimental area for the government's total war, with testing the effectiveness of the Alsa Masa vigilante force as the main subject of the experiment. According to Alsa Masa legend, the group was born in April 1986 when residents of a Davao City shanty town known as Agdao rose up and killed an NPA rebel. This revised history of the group fits the LIC strategy of making it appear that an insurgency is collapsing due to popular discontent.

In reality, the first group to call themselves Alsa Masa are members of a private gang under the control of a corrupt local government official named Wilfredo "Baby" Aquino (who was later killed by the NPA). The gang had close connections with the military (1984-86) for whom they served as informers and partners in crime syndicates. The gang was reorganised in late 1987 by Davao City Metropolitan District Commander Lieutenant Colonel Frank Calida to assist the military in counterinsurgency. The Regional Special Action Force (RSAF) of the military works closely with the Alsa Masa in moving into new communities and providing them with logistical and back up tactical support.[15] In addition to tactical support, the military have also supplied arms and financial support to Alsa Masa.

The relationship between the military and Alsa Masa was summed up in a 1987 interview by then Secretary of Defense Rafael Ileto, who stated:

> Alsa Masa…is not part of the military so we're not accountable for them. Lt. Col. Franco Calida is not leading the Alsa Masa. He's indirectly cooperating. He's not in control. If an Alsa Masa kills a man, Calida cannot be tried for command responsibility. They're not integrated into the military, they're ordinary citizens.[16]

Alsa Masa essentially provided the military with an organization to carry out its "dirty war," but for which it could claim it had no responsibility.

From these modest beginnings in Davao, Alsa Masa, with the assistance of the military and other groups, organized itself into a nation-wide network. In Mindanao, the group serves as an umbrella to a host of anti-communist and fanatical religious groups, including many dating back to the Marcos era such as Sagrado Corazon Senor or Tadtad, Remnants of God, Guerrero de Jesus and the Philippine Benevolent Missionaries Association, with the latter group having been trained by the military under Marcos for the purpose of assisting in fighting the NPA in both the South in Mindanao and in the North in Kalinga Apayao province.

These various vigilante groups are the conduits of anti-communist propaganda at the grassroots level and are an essential component in the psychological warfare being waged against what is considered the mass base of the insurgents. Alsa Masa members, accompanied by military officers and local government officials, often lecture community residents on the evils of communism and the need to organize themselves against it. Pressure is put on residents to either join Alsa Masa or to allow an Alsa Masa detachment to be set up in their neighbourhood. The message is always clear: "no one can remain neutral."[17]

In Davao City, Alsa Masa members have gone from community to community telling residents that there is no longer any middle ground, and that they must either support the activities of Alsa Masa or be considered communists.[18] Those who do not wish to join are sometimes forced by threats on their lives or the lives of their families. People refusing to join have had their houses marked with a red X and later had their residences strafed. The aim of this ideological warfare is to create total polarization within targeted communities.

This process of polarization has been further facilitated by vigilante control over the airwaves in Davao City. The best known Alsa Masa broadcaster is DXOW Radio's Jun Pala. Pala, a student of the Moonie's CAUSA anti-communist seminars in Manila, went as far as threatening top-ranking government officials, and with punishment if they do not toe Alsa Masa's line. In one case, two members of Davao City Council (Luz Iligan and Dante Escalante) were warned over the air by Pala that "they would have their brains scattered on the ground"[19] after arguing unsuccessfully that Alsa Masa should not be given the $11,000 it had requested from the city. Pala was later given an award by the city government for his "promotion of democracy and freedom."[20]

Under these circumstances, legitimate dissent has become subversive and legal organizations are targeted as communist fronts. Certain groups have been singled out as targets for vigilante actions. The list includes members of the League of Filipino students, BAYAN (a nationalist political alliance), the KMU (a labour centre), GABRIELA (a coalition of women's groups), ACT (Alliance of Concerned Teachers), as well as a number of other cause-oriented and church-based organizations.

The Catholic Church, in particular, is viewed with suspicion by the vigilantes. Lieutenant Colonel Frank Calida boasted that "there are almost no communists left in Davao City today...just the priests and nuns, and we'll go after them next."[21] Certain Catholic orders such as "Redempterrorists" (sic) and Carmelites have been singled out by the military and vigilantes as fronts for communist activities. While the church was singled out as a target by the vigilantes, one of their more notable supporters in Davao City was Archbishop Antonio Mabutas who, in 1988, expressed fear of the consequences should the vigilantes be disbanded.[22]

Even attempts at self-reliant development such as cooperatives fall under the rubric of subversion. In the small fishing village of Punta Dumalag south of Davao City, Alsa Masa moved in and dynamited the community fishing project, destroyed a soap-making operation, and removed all medicine and equipment from the community health clinic. Clearly, the aim was to destroy the unity and independence of the community.

Vigilante groups outside of Davao City have undergone a process of development similar to that of Alsa Masa. The much heralded Nakasaka[23] of Digos has been portrayed by the military and local government as a spontaneous movement of the people.[24] While members of fanatical religious groups such as the Tadtad have voluntarily joined the vigilantes, in reality coercion and threats have been the main methods of recruiting members. The major pressure to organize at the local level, in Mindanao, has come from military and civilian officials and in Negros from large landowners and sugar planters.

The examples of Alsa Masa and Nakasaka clearly contradict Aquino's version of the vigilante phenomenon as a grassroots anti-communist, hegemonic movement. These cases demonstrate that the so-called people's uprising consists primarily of a core group of criminal gangs and fanatical religious groups (previously utilized by the Marcos regime). The organization and endorsement of these groups by the Aquino government and the military reflect state attempts to privatize the conflict, and in doing so, bringing the war against the insurgents to the civilian population.

Foreign Friends?

The privatization of the Philippine state's anti-communist campaign has been bolstered by assistance from numerous private foreign-based organizations and individuals, some of whom are directly linked to the U.S. administration. This in many ways reflects the emerging "two-track" strategy in U.S. foreign policy involving, on the one hand, public support by the U.S. government (through the military, United States Information Service [USIS], the U.S. Agency for International Development [US-AID], and the Peace Corps[25]) and on the other hand, the use of private citizens and/or institutions to carry out foreign policy decisions.

It can be argued that the participation of non-government actors in U.S. counterinsurgency work is nothing new, since involving private individuals and companies in CIA operations has been part of the covert foreign policy tradition. Traditional counterinsurgency assistance from the Non-Government Organization (NGO) community has focused on the provision of development aid and institutional support in areas where insurgency is the strongest. In the Philippines, this institutional support had always been provided by the church and more recently through the U.S. labour movement.

The "official"[26] labour movement in the Philippines, known as the Trade Union Congress of the Philippines (TUCP), provided a conduit for more private aid in the struggle against communism. The primary external supporters of the TUCP are the International Confederation of Free Trade Unions (ICFTU) and the American Asia Free Labour Institute (AAFLI). The ICFTU is a strongly anti-communist international alliance of national labour organizations representing labour movements in "capitalist" countries (e.g., Canadian Labour Congress [CLC], American Federation of Labour-Congress of Industrial Organizations [AFL-CIO]) and provides international support and recognition for the TUCP. According to a U.K. Trade Union Delegation to the Philippines,[27] the AAFLI channels funds from the CIA and the AFL-CIO to the TUCP. According to the director of the AFFLI, Charles Gray, its programs "have evolved beyond traditional trade union activities" to encompass development and organizational activities in "just those areas where the communists are most active, such as Mindanao, Negros, Iloilo, and Cebu."[28] In evolving beyond the traditional boundaries of trade union activities, the TUCP has come to play a very active role in supporting the LIC campaign now being waged in the Philippines.

While elements of the labour movement in the Philippines (through the support of the AFL-CIO, CLC, and ICFTU) continue to provide traditional support to counterinsurgency by undermining more militant unions, other private elements have become much more involved in the organization of military operations directly engaged in rollback. The direct involvement of a network of private individuals in the organization and financial support of military ventures provides a marked departure from previous forms of support. This network has provided certain members of the U.S. administration with the ability to carry out and direct a covert foreign policy agenda.

One of the main links between the U.S. administration and a privatized version of U.S. foreign policy has been General John Singlaub. Singlaub came to prominence in 1984 when he assisted Oliver North (then of the National Security Council) in organizing a network of corporate and individual sponsors for the Nicarauguan contras, effectively privatizing U.S. aid to circumvent U.S. congressional restrictions on administration funding of the contras. Not only does Singlaub sit on a National Security Council Advisory Committee, he is also a member of the

U.S. Special Warfare Advisory Group which helped formulate the LIC doctrine. Moreover, his role as U.S. organizer of the World Anti-Communist League and former President of that world body provides an important link between official U.S foreign policy and the unofficial privatized version which developed under the Reagan administration.

General Singlaub's work in the Philippines has centred on the organization of both government and non-government counterinsurgency operations. To train the New Armed Forces of the Philippines (NAFP) in unconventional counterinsurgency tactics, Singlaub reportedly recruited 37 mercenaries for work in the Philippines.[29] In addition, he was reportedly working with Negros landowners encouraging them to build up their own private armies to support government efforts in fighting the NPA. In his attempts to facilitate LIC, Singlaub has received assistance from a variety of U.S.-based right-wing and fundamentalist organizations (i.e., World Anti-Communist League, Christian Anti-Communist Crusade, Unification Church).

Fundamentalism and Low Intensity Conflict

Fundamentalist groups were first recognized as an important ally of U.S. foreign policy in the late 1960s, a period when an increasingly activist liberation-oriented Catholic Church had shaken the confidence of American strategists. In 1970, a special foreign policy commission for Latin America headed by Nelson Rockefeller concluded that "the Catholic Church has ceased to be an ally in whom the United States can have confidence."[30] Rockefeller's commission further recommended that to counter this situation, the government should promote "an extensive campaign with the National Security Council with the aim of propagating Protestant Churches and conservative sects in Latin America."[31]

The fundamentalist sects are seen as useful allies because of the anti-communist xenophobia which many of these groups exhibit. According to Peter Brock, an Australian working with the National Council of Churches of the Philippines, the fundamentalist ideology sees the world in absolute and deterministic terms: "The world is black and white, good and evil, East and West, communism and democracy." In the Philippines, major fundamentalist groups such as the Christian Anti-Communist Crusade (an affiliate of the World Anti-Communist League), the Asian

Ecumenical Inter-Faith Council (a local affiliate of the Unification Church), Mormons, the Moral Majority, the Campus Crusade for Christ, and the Opus Dei of the Catholic Church, have all been involved in major propaganda offensives aimed at countering the growth of liberation theology.[32]

Psychological manipulation through propaganda and the fanning of anti-communist hysteria to prevent the revolutionary movement from gaining ground is imperative and probably the most important component needed in setting the stage for LIC implementation. According to one report, Christian fundamentalist groups have facilitated the proliferation of anti-communist vigilante groups such as the Alsa Masa, and have been a major sponsor of anti-communist conferences in the Philippines. The major fundamentalist groups that have made inroads are the Unification Church and Christian Anti-Communist Crusade (CACC).

One of the major sources of funding for the World Anti-Communist League (WACL) is the Unification Church. The church, through its political arm CAUSA International, has taken an active role in promoting anti-communism. According to CAUSA's own literature, the organization was formed to assist in the development of an "ideological offensive against communism."[33] Since 1980, CAUSA has been active in Latin America, conducting its ideological work primarily in South America; particularly Uruguay, Paraguay, Chile, and Bolivia where it has purchased newspapers, along with radio and television stations, and in Central America among the contras when they were an active force.[34]

In the Philippines, the Asian Ecumenical Inter-Faith Council, a front for CAUSA International, has been very active in creating links with other conservative religious groups and sponsoring anti-communist activities. It has set up other local affiliates such as the Spiritual Action Movement Foundation Inc, with the former Vice-President's wife Celia Diaz-Laurel as its leader, and cultivated links with the Baptist Missionary affiliate Alliance for Democracy and Morality (ADAM). In addition, CAUSA International sponsored two major "anti-communist" conferences at the Manila hotel in October 1986 and March 1987, the latter attended by then Vice-President Salvador Laurel.

CAUSA's work in the Philippines has also received support from U.S. government agencies such as the USIS, which has served as a conduit for the groups's anti-communist literature and a sponsor of CAUSA's anti-communist seminars through its offices in Cebu. Other U.S. government agencies provide assistance for CAUSA's educational campaigns. One of CAUSA's leaders, Bo Hi Pak, revealed that his group receives funding from the CIA.[35] In addition to assisting CAUSA, it has been reported[36] that the CIA covertly sponsored the first national conference of anti-communist organizations held at the Trade Union Congress of the Philippines headquarters in February 1987.

Another affiliate of both Singlaub and the WACL is Australian Dr. John Whitehall, Vice President of the Christian Anti-Communist Crusade and member of WACL. Whitehall has reportedly conducted some fourteen anti-communist tours through the Philippines, many of which were arranged by the Armed Forces of the Philippines,[37] thus revealing the close link between these two groups. In July 1986, the group met with the leadership of the Armed Forces of the Philippines (including General Ramos) and planned coordinated activities which included four CACC visits to the Philippines in 1986 and contacts with Alsa Masa, the main vigilante group.[38]

The main Philippine co-worker in this fundamentalist anti-communist network is Jun Alcover, a baptist minister. Alcover appears as a unifying thread in the multi-sectoral coalition which makes up the anti-communist network. Aside from Alcover's religious connection, he is a Lieutenant-Colonel in the AFP, and he broadcasts anti-communist propaganda over a radio station owned by the Trade Union Congress of the Philippines. In addition, Alcover is a national organiser of Alsa Masa[39] and a leader of another vigilante group known as KADRE (*Kalihukan sa Democratikong Reporma* or Movement for Democratic Reform). Alcover and KADRE have been active in counterinsurgency work at Atlas Mines near Cebu City.

The case of Atlas Mines demonstrates the interconnection between different elements of this private network, in particular the AFL-CIO supported TUCP and the vigilantes. Here, a TUCP affiliate lost a certification bid at Asia's largest copper mine to the more militant KMU-affiliated Panaghiusa sa mga Mamumuo sa Atlas (PAMA-KMU) in 1985 to represent 10,000 workers at the mine. Following their defeat, the TUCP joined forces with the company and local government officials to try to break the union, through the use of vigilante groups. The company permitted ten supporters of the TUCP union to undergo paid leave for military training. These ten then formed the basis of the KADRE vigilante group, which led a campaign of terror. The vigilantes branded PAMA as "communist" thus making all its supporters targets of harassments. The terror resulted in the deaths of ten local members of the miners union[40] and the strafing of its union office. This local vigilante group has received the support of the mayor, Elisa San Juan, who is the wife of an Atlas Mines executive and regional chairperson of the extreme rightist group Peoples Alliance Against Communism.[41] Additional support has been provided by the local radio station (which is run by the TUCP and supported by the Friedrich Ebert Stiftung agency in West Germany).[42]

The main objective of this campaign of terror was to undermine support for the miners' union in a 1989 certification election. In spite of the reign of terror, PAMA won the March 21st certification vote with 68.3 percent of the vote, the vigilante-backed Movement for Democratic Labour Organizations (MODELO) headed by the same Jun Alcover received 20 percent of the votes.[43] When it was apparent that PAMA would win the vote, the vigilantes tried to have the election cancelled and twice forced postponements through intimidation. The response to the postponements was work slowdowns by both the miners and supervisory personnel which, along with outside pressure, eventually forced a vote. In a victory statement, the local president Antonio Cuison said that the results "proved the Atlas workers reject the anti-labour schemes of vigilante-backed yellow unions and...that the workers have frustrated the Low Intensity Conflict experiment of the Aquino regime."[44] While the victory of the workers at Atlas Mines indicates that it is possible to resist the onslaught of Low Intensity Warfare, the experience of the progressive movement in other areas has been somewhat mixed in the face of this terror.

The Impact on the Progressive Forces

A number of factors have combined to either temper or intensify the impact of the vigilante terror on progressive forces in the Philippines. These factors include: the relative strength of the progressive forces in a particular area; the level of internal consolidation; the geographic location (urban versus rural); and whether the particular organization is underground or a legal, open mass movement. These factors, in addition to the intensity with which an area was targeted, have combined to produce differential impacts. While the LIC program had a national focus, repression was most intense on the islands of Negros and Mindanao, particularly Davao City; areas where the progressive movement had made the most rapid advances in the final years of the dictatorship.

Low Intensity Conflict was designed primarily to undercut support for the underground. The main targets of this strategy were the Communist Party of the Philippines, its military arm, the New Peoples Army (NPA) and the National Democratic Front (NDF). These forces had led the struggle against the Marcos dictatorship from 1972 to 1986.[45] They were engaged not only in an anti-dictatorship struggle but also in a national democratic struggle against imperialism and the feudal landholding structure in the country. After the dictatorship, these organizations became the target of intensive repression because they continued to struggle for national democracy.

The impact of the LIC strategy on the underground movement has varied from one area to the next depending on the level of the organization's consolidation. Since martial law was declared in September 1972, the Communist Party has undertaken the building of guerrilla zones at strategic points in all major islands of the country. Within these zones, the underground has sought to build stable guerrilla bases and basic components of a revolutionary government through which they provide basic social services such as health, education and a system of justice. While consolidated guerrilla zones have been effected from time to time by direct military assaults (most notably in Negros and the Cordillera in Northern Luzon), the impact of LIC has not been strong in these areas, as the counterrevolutionary forces lack a base from which to organize.

LIC has had its greatest impact in the "white areas," where the political terrain is constantly contested by the government and the national democratic movement. While there are pockets of political conflict through-out the country, most of the counterinsurgency was focused on larger urban centres such as Manila and Davao, or on large work sites such as Atlas Mines, LADECO and large sugar haciendas on the island of Negros.

Davao City — A Case Study of LIC

The left's biggest urban advance and the scene of the most intensive LIC effort was Davao City in Mindanao. Here, the NPA took full advantage of such factors as favourable terrain, worsening economic crisis, growing social unrest and a developing political upsurge to rapidly advance the guerrilla warfare and the mass movement into the urban areas of the Philippines' third largest city. From 1983 to the middle of 1985, the armed struggle in the city reached an unprecedented scale. Sparrow units (three member teams of urban guerrillas) would emerge from the slums to attack police and military forces. The level of organization and military operations was so advanced that it became unsafe for the military to leave their barracks unless in force.

Revolutionary mass organizations like the Kabataang Makabayan (KM) and the Kalihokan sa Rebolusyonaryong Mamumuo (KRM) expanded their membership among the youth and working class respectively. The Christians for National Liberation (CNL), the underground national democratic organization in the church sector, began organizing chapters throughout the city. Cells of the NDF were organized among the middle forces in many business offices and firms.[46]

Davao's largest slum, Agdao, became known as "Nicaragdao" and another barrio called Ma-a was called "Ma-anagua" indicating the extent of revolutionary control in these areas.[47] Slum dwellers reportedly flocked to the underground movement in this period, "some out of political conviction, and others to belong to something exciting."[48] During this period, the masses in the city launched numerous protest actions punctuated by general strikes, while at the same time the local elite made accommodations with the underground movement or sold their assets and left.

Two interrelated problems emerged in 1984-85 that slowed the growth of the revolutionary movement. The first problem was a failure to consolidate new members. The second was infiltration by Deep Penetration Agents (DPAs). The consolidation problem emerged from the backlog of new recruits in the Party and the mass organizations, due in part to the tremendous growth of the movement, and in part to a refocusing of priorities. The revolutionary forces had become too preoccupied with the actual intensification of military actions and mass campaigns to give full attention to the issue of political consolidation of its membership. The problem of enemy infiltration was detected in the middle of 1985. This problem of DPAs was said to have been "overestimated and mishandled to the point of causing dislocations, confusion and demoralization within the revolutionary ranks."[49]

The DPA problem was dealt with through a massive purge of Party members in both the city and countryside. According to one analyst, by the time the campaign was stopped, only 3,000 of the 9,000 members in the Mindanao CPP remained.[50] It is believed that 300 persons were killed. The rest fled to other areas, were reassigned or simply stopped operating. It took until 1988 to once again reach 6,000 Party members in Mindanao. The result was a weakening of the revolutionary movement in Davao City. The combination of the paranoia caused by the enemy infiltration and the poor consolidation of new forces within the movement made it difficult for the underground to deal with the rapidly changing political terrain.

The Aquino Regime

When Aquino took power, those who had been politically involved on the basis of an anti-Marcos, anti-dictatorship struggle felt there was no longer a need for a revolution. This change on the political terrain resulted in a decrease in membership of organizations belonging to the middle sectors, including women, students, professionals, the church and artists. The loss of these articulate, well-connected middle forces was serious, as they had provided an important buffer to human rights violations for the other sectors.

During the first year of the Aquino regime, the Party leadership decided to slow the armed struggle, while they assessed the new political leadership and the mood of the masses. There was indecisiveness in the underground movement brought about by internal debates regarding the new regime and the democratic possibilities it offered. In addition, the organization in Davao City was still recovering from the dissension brought about by the problem of its handling of DPAs. It was in this context that the underground faced a rising tide of vigilante and military assaults. Soon after the breakdown of the cease-fire talks between the NDF and the government in early 1987,[51] President Aquino launched the "total war" against the NDF. OPLAN EAGLE[52] was launched by the regional command in the Davao City area. The counterinsurgency plan consisted of the following elements: 1) Detachment Building: which included the establishment of military checkpoints and detachments in all of the 72 communities in Davao City — in poor urban areas, the military posts were doubled; 2) Armed Civil Defense Groups, also known as vigilantes, were formed to drive a wedge between the revolutionary forces and civilians; 3) Psychological Operations including a massive propaganda campaign through the media (Jun Pala) and other sources; 4) Civic and Humanitarian Assistance, such as the visit of the U.S. hospital ship USNS Mercy to Davao City, which provided free medical assistance to Davao residents; and 5) Assassination of selected targets by counterinsurgency forces.[53]

Response to LIC — Tactical Retreat from the City

The underground movement was basically unprepared for the level and intensity of the counterinsurgency campaign. The partisans (urban guerrillas) and underground organizations responded to LIC by withdrawing from active work in the city. The strategic retreat from Davao City that took place in February 1987, however, did not result in a total withdrawal.[54] The number of cadres decreased but skeleton forces were maintained in the communities until such time as conditions were favourable for recovery.

The groups which suffered the greatest setbacks from LIC were the basic sectors, the urban poor, the workers and the peasants. The most damaging effects were felt in urban poor areas which went into a lull as there was a complete withdrawal of revolutionaries from previous strongholds like Agdao and Ma-a. The underground work of the KRM within the trade unions was also severely affected by LIC. In some factories, underground unions had already been established, but these were abandoned. The peasants in Davao City were hit hard in 1987.[55] The strategy in the rural areas was both "high" and "low" intensity as the military conducted bombing campaigns on some of the villages around the city, in addition to the vigilante terror. While the effects of this campaign were damaging in the "white areas", in areas of the city where revolutionary government had already been established, the effects of LIC were said to be minimal.[56]

Overall underground organizational work in the city was continued by some of the member organizations of the NDF, including the KM (youth), CNL (church), and MAKIBAKA (women) during this period. The basic strategy for those who remained active was to work within the vigilante groups if necessary, win over those who had been forced to join the vigilantes, and neutralize the organization and isolate more dangerous elements. The leading proponents of terrorism within the vigilante groups were selectively targeted by the NPA, but such actions were tempered by vigilante reprisals against leaders of open mass organizations.[57]

In September 1988, the NPA attacked a group of vigilantes in Davao and killed their leader known as Commander Morris. Following this attack, the vigilantes issued death threats to progressive groups, most notably the KMU, to avenge the death of their leader. A few weeks later, Oscar Bantayan, a KMU national council member, was shot dead by five members of the Alsa Masa.[58] While there is no clear connection between these events, the threat of retaliation was one factor that curtailed NPA military operations during this period in Davao City.

Unlike the underground, the legal mass movements did not simply pull out of the city. These organizations continued to advocate a national democratic agenda through militant struggle short of armed rebellion. The militant stand of these organizations made them and their members open targets for intimidation, harassment and in some cases assassination. Among those assassinated in 1987 by vigilantes were Maria Luisen, an urban poor leader killed by Alsa Masa; and Peter Alderite, a labour organizer at the Lapanday Development Corporation (LADECO). Alderite was hacked to death and decapitated by vigilantes who paraded his head around like a trophy. A number of other union officials at LADECO were also killed by vigilantes. Fredrico Fuentes was shot dead on December 10, 1986 in Davao City while attending a rally commemorating international human rights day,[59] and in 1988 Danilo Martinez was killed. In the face of this terror, the work of organizations such as the KMU, Bayan, and Gabriela continued, but at a lower level.

Recovery and Renewed Growth

Since 1987, the revolutionary forces in Mindanao have recovered from the internal problems and damage wrought by intense enemy attacks. In May 1987, a Party committee called the Special White Area Team (SWAT) was formed to oversee the recovery of the Davao area. The first target for recovery were areas in the surrounding countryside which served as a base for moving back into the urban areas.

An initial sign of recovery was a very successful 1988 national general strike to protest oil price increases in Davao City. Many community chapters of Alsa Masa joined up with militant workers and other sectoral organizations to bring transportation to a halt for one day. Alsa Masa members also launched protests with militant workers' organizations on economic issues such as demolition of squatter settlements, housing for the urban poor, and land. By 1989, partisan operations, the building of revolutionary organizations, and "united front" work with non-underground organizations were all moving forward. Many Alsa Masa members were said to have secretly returned to the revolutionary movement.[60]

In Davao City, partisan military operations have been launched since the start of the recovery, but have not reached previous levels. The NPA claim to be more discriminating in their choice of targets than they were in the past. The main military targets in the recovery period have been the hardcore elements of Alsa Masa and other rightist vigilante groups, the military, government officials with "blood debts to the people," and foreign nationals involved in counterinsurgency operations.[61] The military operations now undertaken are less dramatic because the underground partisans are aware of the impact their operations have had on legal aboveground groups. There had been some negative publicity associated with their actions in the past, suggesting that they were out of control, killing indiscriminately. An indication of the impact of renewed activity was the declaration by the Armed Forces of the Philippines in 1990 that the southern partisans were active once again.

According to an internal assessment, the mass base in Davao City recovered in early 1991.[62] Work is presently under way to reactivate abandoned underground trade unions. Organizational strength, however, has yet to reach previous levels.[63] In spite of this, between October 1990 and January 1991, there were four general strikes in Davao which is a clear indication of recovery in this sector. Only one of the poor urban areas in the city had not been recovered as of February 1991, but the problem was not considered serious.

The recovery of urban areas was made possible by advances in organizing work, as the economic crisis continued to intensify under the Aquino government. In addition, struggles over the distribution of protection money and the personal ambitions of competing leaders have split vigilante groups. The noted propagandist, Jun Pala, went into hiding in 1990 after a struggle with Colonel Calida, who was subsequently transferred to western Mindanao. The checkpoints once staffed by vigilantes throughout the city now sit abandoned. The only apparent presence of the vigilantes are their painted slogans on walls around the city.

Conclusion

There is overwhelming evidence that the Aquino regime has orchestrated an anti-communist campaign of physical and psychological terror against its civilian population. As a result of the military's inability to put down the insurgency on its own, the state opted for a new strategy which attempts to bring civil society and many of its institutions into the mainstream of the conflict. Central to the government's program was the formation of vigilante groups through the military and Ministry of Local Government. The Aquino government, for its part, gave a blanket endorsement to the vigilantes and facilitated their development, utilizing existing networks such as criminal gangs and fanatical cults to buttress military operations within local communities. The government's sponsorship of the vigilante groups has brought ideological warfare, focused on the elimination of dissent and the political left, one step forward by introducing a comprehensive program of militarization into the fabric of local community life.

This campaign of total war has been premised on bringing the convictions and resources of the private sector and private individuals into the conflict. The anti-communist network has played a fundamental role in establishing the conditions for launching grassroots warfare. In the Philippines, this network of private individuals and institutions has been central to the militarization of the grassroots in anti-communist propaganda campaigns, which have polarized local communities. Foreign-based fundamentalist religious groups and foreign nationals have facilitated the formation of vigilante squads.

This phenomenon clearly reflects a developing trend of incorporating a broad range of individuals into covert aspects of U.S. foreign policy initiatives. The cases of Nicaragua and the Philippines demonstrate that these networks are important to the operationalization of a new foreign policy based on Low Intensity Conflict. In setting up networks of the New Right to carry out these objectives, it is possible to circumvent the roadblocks (e.g., Congress) to the reactionary rollback agenda.

While important links between the religious right, other private institutions, and LIC have been established, further research is required to more successfully combat the evolving Global Contra War. The example of Davao City indicates that this strategy provided only temporary setbacks for the underground and popular forces. In all likelihood the damage would have been less severe if the underground had not been suffering from such severe internal problems in the first place. These problems provided the conditions for the maximum impact of Low Intensity Conflict. This conjuncture of events gave the impression that the underground had been forced out of the city. In effect, the vigilantes simply moved into the spaces previously occupied by the underground as its organization collapsed because of its own mistakes. Much to its credit, however, the underground was able for the most part to overcome its serious organizational problems and move back into the city.

Despite serious setbacks under the Aquino regime, the revolutionary movement remains strong. At present, the Party counts 30-35,000 activists, community and labour leaders, and full-time revolutionaries among its members.[64] The NPA has maintained its fighting force of about 10,000 regulars and has developed larger fighting formations in recent years.[65] The consolidated rural bases have a population of about 750,000, and underground influence extends over another 9,000 to 12,000 barrios with a total population of about 10 million.[66]

The Aquino regime and its U.S. backers have fought a "total war" against the rural bases, the trade unions and other popular forces. But the popular forces have held their ground, and their strength is reflected in official politics. On September 16th, 1991 the Philippine Senate voted on a Treaty of Friendship, Cooperation and Security signed by the Aquino government and the United States in August of 1991. At the heart of the treaty is the question of whether the U.S. lease on the Subic Bay naval base would be renewed after 1992. The base is one of the United States' most important overseas bases. Before the vote Philippine Senate President Jovito Salonga stated: "Today, we have finally summoned the political will to stand up and end 470 years of foreign military presence here."[67] Then 12 of the 23 senators voted against the treaty, which required a two-thirds vote for approval. Some senators saw the vote as an end to Philippine dependency. But Aquino revoked the Senate's notice of termination of the lease on Subic Bay, and extended the U.S. term indefinitely. This action was immediately condemned as unconstitutional.

Despite the financial cost of the loss of the U.S. base, with 40,000 jobs directly tied to its operation, significant popular opinion runs against renewal of the lease, for the U.S. presence also brings with it immeasurable degradation and exploitation of Filipinos. The rising opposition to renewal of the U.S. lease can be seen as an indication of the weakness of the Aquino regime, and the strength of the anti-imperialist and popular forces arrayed against the regime and its U.S. backers. It would appear that Uncle Sam's "new world order" is not assured!

Notes

1. This does not imply that the whole EDSA (People's Power) revolt was an event stage managed to meet U.S. foreign policy objectives. It was clearly a genuine expression of the popular will, which was utilized to meet foreign policy objectives.
2. See the Debates in the *Diliman Review*, 1986-7. The review, published at the University of the Philippines, contains a lively debate among different elements of the Left on the strategic possibilities of legal struggle under the Aquino government.
3. The NDF, established in 1973, is a revolutionary coalition of progressive and nationalist organizations.
4. *Ottawa Citizen*, March, 23, 1987. Quoted from a speech by President Aquino to the graduating class of the Philippine Military Academy.
5. *Justice and Peace Review*, Vol.2 No.4, 1987, p.8.
6. The NPA is the main guerrilla force under the revolutionary coalition of the National Democratic Front. By the military's own estimates, it has reportedly grown to more than 25,000 guerrillas nationwide since its founding in 1969.
7. Suzanne Jonas, *U.S. Policy and the Peace Process: Guatemala and El Salvador* (A Discussion Document), October, 1988.
8. Dr. Sam Sarkesian, "Low-Intensity Conflict: Concepts, Principles and Policy Guidelines," *Air University Review*, Jan-Feb. 1985. Quoted in Reynaldo T. Racaza, *A Global Perspective on Low-Intensity Conflict: Total War at the Grassroots Level*, National Council of Churches Philippines-Human Rights Desk Occasional Papers, 1987, p. 2.
9. *Justice and Peace Review*, Vol 2, No.4, 1987, p. 5.
10. Salvaging is a term used by human rights groups to describe summary execution.

11. *Justice and Peace Review*, Vol 4, No. 2, 1987, p. 8.
12. Ferrer, by coincidence, had served in the 1950s as aide to then Colonel Edward Lansdale, who engineered CIA counterinsurgency efforts against the HUKs (originally an anti-Japanese guerrilla movement).
13. Canada Asia Working Group, *Human Rights in Asia*, Geneva, February, 1988. p.34.
14. Racaza, op cit, p.16.
15. *Kalinangan*, Vol.2, No.2 June 1987, p. 14.
16. Ninotchka Rosca, "Two Views on the Guerrilla War" Interview with General Rafael Ileto (Secretary of National Defense), *Midweek*, Vol.2 No.28, July 1, 1987.
17. Enrique Delacruz, Aida Jordan and Jorge Emmanuel, *Death Squads in the Philippines*, Alliance for Philippine Concerns, 1987. p.10.
18. *Kalinangan*, Vol.2 No.2, June 1987, p.13.
19. Delacruz et al. *Death Squads in the Philippines*, 1987. p.18.
20. Delacruz, op cit, p.31.
21. Bruce Occena, "Aquino Government Shifts to the Right," *Frontline*, April 13, 1987, p.13 cited in Racaza, op cit, p.15.
22. Christians for National Liberation (Davao City), "Pro-Vigilante Bishop" *Midweek*, Vol.3 No.40, September 28, 1988, pp. 35-6.
23. One of the organizers of this group, Douglas Cagas, was lauded by President Aquino for using "People power to bring freedom to our future....without the use of arms."
24. Delacruz, op cit, p.21.
25. Vitan, *Philippine Insight*, September-October, 1986, p.11. reports that the Peace Corps has now deployed volunteers in elementary and local schools "to help local teachers."
26. It is official in the sense that it is the only body recognized by the Philippines government and Western labour organizations such as the ICFTU, CLC, AFL-CIO as representing Philippine labour. In fact, the TUCP was a labour central established by the Marcos regime as an advisory body to facilitate the implementation of government policy.
27. UK Philippines Support Group Trade Union Committee Delegation, *Genuine Trade Unionism in the Philippines*, London, 1985.
28. Walden Bello, *US-Sponsored Low-Intensity Conflict in the Philippines*, Institute for Food and Development Policy, 1989.
29. *Justice and Peace Review*, Vol.2 No.4, 1987. p.4.
30. Rev. Thomas J. Marti, *Fundamentalist Sects and the Political Right*, Manila, Philippines, October, 3, 1986, p.1.
31. Marti, op cit, p.1.
32. *Manila Chronicle*, November, 16, 1987, p.7.
33. Dr. Michael McKale, "CAUSA International and CAUSA USA: Saving the World by Fighting Communism," *CALC Report*, December, 1986, p.8.
34. McKale, op cit, pp.8-10.
35. *Manila Chronicle*, November 16, 1987, p.7.
36. *Justice and Peace Review*, Vol 4, No. 2, 1987, p.7.
37. Peter Brock, "Christian Anti-Communism" *Kalinangan*, June, 1987, p.4.
38. *Kalinangan*, June, 1987.
39. Brock, op cit, p.6.
40. KMU International Department, *Correspondence*, Vol.IV No.4, 1989, p.15 and *Currents*, Canada-Asia Working Group, Vol.10 No.3, October, 1988, p.25.
41. KMU International Department, *Correspondence*, Vol.III No.11, December 1988. p.12.
42. Institute for Labour Research and Documentation, "Philippine Trade Unionism: A Situationer," *Philippine Labour Monitor*, Vol.1 No.2, 1985.

43. KMU International Department, *Correspondence*, Manila, Vol.IV No.4, 1989.
44. *KMU International Department Correspondence*, Vol.4, No.4, May-June 1989, p.16.
45. The Communist Party and the NPA are members of the National Democratic Front, an umbrella grouping of a dozen underground sectoral organizations that constitute the national democratic movement in the Philippines.
46. *Ang Bayan*, "Davao: On the Road to Recovery," Vol.22 No.4, June 1990. p.12.
47. Because these areas were hotbeds of revolutionary activity, they were informally renamed after the Sandinistas took power in Nicaragua.
48. James B. Goodno, *The Philippines: Land of Broken Promises*, 1991, p. 85.
49. *Ang Bayan*, March 1989, p.6.
50. Edicio de la Torre, "Afterword," in B. Pimentel *Rebolusyon!: A Generation of Struggle in the Philippines*, 1991, p.339.
51. These talks broke down as the result of the massacre of 15 peasants, by military personnel on the Mendiola bridge near the Presidential Palace.
52. OPLAN EAGLE was the name of the military operations plan in the Davao region that encompassed both a military and intensive propaganda campaign.
53. Ang Bayan, "Davao: On the Road to Recovery" Vol.22 No.4, June 1990, pp.13-14.
54. Ka Simon, Interview Notes, Davao City, February 20, 1991.
55. Davao City is said to be the largest city in the world in square miles, and much of the city is not in fact urban but remains agricultural land which is worked by peasants.
56. Ka Simon, Interview Notes, Davao City, February 20, 1991.
57. Ibid.
58. KMU International Department, *Action Alert*, November 14, 1988, p.5.
59. Kilusang Mayo Uno, *Action Alert*, November 14, 1988. p.1.
60. *Ang Bayan*, op cit, June 1990. p.17.
61. *Ang Bayan*, op cit, June 1990. p.16.
62. Ka Simon, Interview Notes, February 20, 1991.
63. Ka Simon, Interview Notes, Davao City, February 20, 1991.
64. Goodno, op cit, p.140.
65. Edicio de la Torre, op cit, pp.341-2.
66. Edicio de la Torre, op cit, p.342.
67. John Miller, "Aquino Gives U.S. Base New Lease on Life — For Now," *The Guardian*, Vol. 43, No. 42, October 2, 1991, p. 13.

Chapter Seven

Revolution, Counterrevolution, and Imperialism: La Lucha Continua!*

Dave Broad

*"It was the best of times,
it was the worst of times..."*

On the morning of February 26th, 1990, we learned that, after years of hard work and sacrifice, the Sandinistas and their supporters had lost Nicaragua's second set of free and fair elections (the first were in 1984) to the U.S.-backed Union Nacional de Oposicion (UNO), whose main elements are the liberal and right-wing industrialists and landowners. Close (Chapter Five) has asked if the contras who had been militarily defeated by the Sandinista army, had lost the war but won the election.

The initial shock of the Sandinista defeat was similiar to that many experienced following the U.S. invasion of Grenada in 1983. Looking back, many others will recall Chile in 1973, the Dominion Republic in 1965, et cetera. Bad as the situation is, especially for those directly involved "on the ground," we knew the only way to confront our feelings of defeat and move on was to put this latest defeat in historical perspective. The longer view presented in this chapter shows that political forces have made great advances since the last century, and the "end of history" has *not* been reached.[1] Despite the myopic rush to "inter communism and

---

* This chapter is a revised version of an article published in *Latin American Perspectives*, Fall 1991.

exalt capitalism,"[2] the decline of the latter continues. This might be more obvious if we accept Lenin's view that history moves in a spiral.[3] But many are deceived by U.S. pronouncements of a supposed "new world order" in the wake of the so-called Gulf War with Iraq.

The Longer View

Revolution, counterrevolution, and imperialism are enduring features of the world capitalist system. The transition from feudalism to capitalism in Western Europe occurred as the result of a lengthy struggle between proponents of the new order ("revolutionaries") and those of the old order ("counterrevolutionaries"), with "the masses" pulled in between.[4] And from its inception capitalism has been an imperialist enterprise.[5]

The decline of capitalism also entails a lengthy process of struggle between revolutionaries and counterrevolutionaries.[6] The capitalist world system has experienced two distinct phases of revolution, with 1789 as the watershed. The French Revolution was at once the pinnacle and precipice of capitalism. With its call for "liberty, equality and fraternity," that revolution marked a truly new world order — made all the more urgent by new forms of exploitation and alienation wrought by the Industrial Revolution and subsequent "new imperialism."

The European revolutions of 1848 and the Soviet revolution of 1917 were high points. And despite the history and recent changes in the former Soviet Union, it is clearly inappropriate to conclude, as does Heilbroner: "Less than seventy five years after it officially began, the contest between capitalism and socialism is over — capitalism has won."[7] Such a notion ignores the lengths and uncertainties of previous transitions between social systems, and assumes an end of history. It reveals the old liberal acceptance of capitalism as something "natural" (forgetting that even "nature" changes).

Nonetheless, socialism has had a checkered career. And recent events have thrown all but the most brash ideologues into a state of confusion. We are obviously in one of those historical spaces of great flux. Paul Sweezy has noted: "Certain years go down in history as landmarks — the beginning or end of an era, a major turning point. Such years were 1776, 1789, 1848, 1917, 1939. Nineteen eighty-nine promises to be another worthy of addition to the list."[8] Sweezy is, of course, referring primarily to the changes in Eastern Europe, where the old Stalinist regimes fell in rapid succession, the two Germanies were reunited and where capitalist market reforms appear to be the order of the day. It is also significant that 1989 was the bicentenary of the French Revolution, which was "celebrated" in the West through trivialization and renunciations,[9] as they rush toward the integration of the West European capitalist economies — "Europe 1992."

The year 1989 marked big changes in the Third World as well — a turning point in the struggle between revolutionaries and counterrevolutionaries, capped by the 1990 electoral defeat of the Sandinistas in Nicaragua. There has, in fact, been a significant alteration in post-World War II relations with, some would argue, the disappearance of the "Vietnam Syndrome."[10] After the military defeat of the U.S. in Vietnam in the mid-1970s, U.S. popular opinion and the element of Soviet power constrained the interventionist tendencies of the U.S. It would seem that these constraints are weakening — there being, for example, a low level of U.S. public opposition to the invasion of Panama and so-called Gulf War, and now that the former Soviet Union no longer poses itself as an international counterbalance to U.S. hegemony. The fallout from the recent attempted coup in the Soviet Union seems to have settled that issue, assured its reintegration with the breakaway States into the capitalist world system, and left even Cuba out in the cold.

Low Intensity Conflict?

Some writers attribute the recent U.S. successes to the Pentagon's strategy of "low-intensity conflict" (LIC).[11] In the wake of its defeat in Vietnam, which was accompanied by a global mood of anti-imperialism, U.S. rulers looked for more covert forms of intervention. What became official policy included psychological warfare (trying to win the "hearts and minds" of the masses); the use of economic levers (embargoes, aid); "privatizing" counterrevolutions; arming surrogate fighters ("contras"); and constructing democratic facades in official politics. It might be argued, on the other hand, that LIC is not really a strategy, so much as a group of ad hoc measures which have had varying degrees of success. First, we should note that overt intervention has never been far beneath the surface, rearing its ugly head in Grenada (1983), Panama (1989), and more recently Iraq(1991). Moreover, use of U.S. "advisers," pilots, and military aid in various conflicts amounts to de facto intervention. Not all military attempts to overthrow regimes have succeeded even in the short run, however. The Nicaraguan contras, whom Ronald Reagan called "the moral equivalent of our Founding Fathers," could not muster the civilian support to wage a real insurrectionary war. Little wonder, for they proved themselves to be simply a band of mercenaries, capable of attacking only co-operatives, medical centers, and schools.[12] In Mozambique, the people call the Resistencia Nacional Mozambicana (RENAMO/MNR) contras "bandits."[13]

But contra forces have contributed to imperialist attempts at military and economic destabilization.[14] The revolutionary regimes and peoples have been steadily harassed and driven to pour more and more money, time, energy, and lives into fending off contra incursions. The Sandinista State ended up spending half its budget on defeating the contras. And it is generally recognized that the Sandinista army and militias did militarily defeat the contras, but at such a cost that they lost the 1990 election to the U.S. supported opposition. After nearly a decade of war and economic embargo, the Nicaraguan people voted for a promise of peace and prosperity. According to Sandinista leader Daniel Ortega: "The U.S. gave Nicaraguans the option that if they voted for the Sandinistas the war would continue, the embargo would be maintained, and the economic situation would continue to be disastrous. On the other hand, if they voted for the other option, the war would end and the economic situation would improve."[15] The hearts and minds of the people were not won. Their resistance was ground down.

In Mozambique, the Frente de Libertaçao de Mozambique (FRELIMO) has been forced to make concessions to the International Monetary Fund (IMF) and has gone so far as to stop calling itself "Marxist-Leninist." In Angola the State has done likewise and, as in Nicaragua, has been forced into elections with its contra opponents.[16] And the power that is bequeathed to the contra forces, from Angola to Mozambique to Nicaragua, forces the new regimes to negotiate (generally with little success) with their own torturers.[17]

In cases such as El Salvador and Guatemala, where revolutionary forces have not gained power, the imperialist strategy has involved a shift toward democratic facelifts. If you are trying to win hearts and minds in a war of "democracy" (read capitalism) against "communism," it is hard to justify support for military dictatorships. Throughout Latin America, in fact, we have seen a shift toward "democratic openings."[18] Herman and Brodhead discuss the use of what they label "demonstration elections"from the time of the Vietnam War.[19] The U.S. government has promoted *controlled* elections as a way to co-opt local dissent and to sell their support for counterrevolutionary States both to the international community and to the U.S. public. But these electoral processes are so controlled that the left is excluded and liberal dissenters are co-opted. Such elections are, I have argued elsewhere,[20] not synonymous with but are rather an impediment to democracy, although they have some unintended consequences. The late Guilluermo Ungo of El Salvador's Frente Democrático Revolucionario (FDR) once remarked that the greatest impact of LIC was that it had produced "low intensity solidarity." Indeed, my own experience as a solidarity activist has shown that it is easier to organize and mobilize around a direct intervention, or threat thereof, than to maintain energies and interest over long periods of counterrevolution as usual. It would thus not be surprising if the "Vietnam Syndrome" has begun to erode. But it should well be remembered, despite these apparent setbacks, that demonstration elections are in the end a product of anti-imperialist and revolutionary struggles. In that sense, they are concessions to *real* demands for democracy. They signal the successes and strengths of opposition and popular forces. And the "democratic openings" do offer a further window of opportunity for *real* democratic forces to mobilize after years of repression.

To repeat, LIC should not be seen as something new. Progress has always gone in cycles of varying intensity, and counterrevolution has incorporated both reform and repression or the carrot and the stick. The Bolshevik revolution was greeted with direct intervention, economic embargo, and "contra" opposition ("white terror"),[21] while the wave of attendant revolutions in neighbouring countries had to confront both right-wing repression and the counterrevolutionary stances of social democratic labour and political leaders.[22] And while the former head of the U.S. Southern Command in Panama, General Fred Woerner, has declared that a military victory for the counterrevolution in El Salvador is impossible,[23] the U.S. invasions of Panama and Iraq should remind us that the use of military intervention has not been forsaken ("high intensity conflict") in the "right" circumstances. For those who think the leopard might change its spots, Forkin has provided a list of U.S. interventions from the mid-1800s to the present (see also Chapter One):

> Afghanistan: 1981-present; Angola: 1984-present; Brazil: 1964; Cambodia: 1969, 1970, 1975; Chad: 1982; Chile: 1891, 1973; China: 1900, 1927, 1945-49; Colombia: 1868, 1873, 1895, 1901, 1902, 1928; Cuba: 1848, 1851, 1898-1902, 1906-09, 1912,1917-23, 1933, 1961, 1962; Dominican Republic: 1903, 1904, 1911,1914,1916-24, 1965; El Salvador: 1932, 1981-present; Grenada: 1983; Guatemala: 1923, 1954; Haiti: 1888, 1905, 1915-34; Honduras: 1896, 1903, 1905, 1907, 1909, 1910, 1911, 1912, 1919, 1924, 1925, 1985-86; Indonesia: 1965; Iran: 1953, 1980; Japan: 1853-54; Korea: 1950-53 (or perhaps-present); Laos: 1960, 1971,1977; Lebanon: 1958,1982-84; Libya: 1981, 1986; Mexico: 1846-48,1913-14, 1916; Nicaragua: 1833, 1855-57, 1860, 1894, 1896, 1899, 1909, 1910, 1911, 1912-25, 1926-33, 1983-present; Panama: 1856, 1865, 1885, 1903, 1904, 1908, 1912, 1918, 1925, 1964, 1989; Peru: 1835; Philippines: 1898-1946; Puerto Rico: 1899-present; Soviet Union: 1918-20; Thailand: 1962; Uruguay: 1855, 1858, 1868; Vietnam 1954-75; Zaire: 1960, 1964.[24]

The long history of U.S. interventions worldwide was surely not lost on Nicaraguan voters, who elected the U.S.-backed candidates in the immediate wake of the invasion of Panama.

A Social Democratic Interlude?

But Nicaraguans are not experiencing a return to the status quo ante. Kahn notes how

> Gramsci wrote...that in periods of static equilibrium in the relationship of forces, both sides acquiesce in a dictator to put a halt to unending and unresolvable civil strife. According to Gramsci, who follows Marx in this observation, such a dictator can lend support, as much as the relationship of forces allows, to either the progressive or reactionary forces.[25]

If we substitute "democrat" (read liberal cum social democrat) for "dictator" in this quote, we get an approximation of the present situation in Central America. In Nicaragua both sides have acquiesced in the "democracy" of the bourgeois opposition. In El Salvador, there are serious negotiations between the ruling class and the opposition forces, with even the Frente Farabundo Martí para la Liberación Nacional (FMLN) talking about the need for a negotiated settlement and a pluralist politics.[26] What are the prospects for compromise?

In Nicaragua, the Frente Sandinista de Liberación Nacional (FSLN) took 41 percent of the vote in 1990 and is the best organized political movement in the country. There the relationship of forces means that the "democrat," whose own alliance is a fractured one,[27] must *gain* support from the progressive forces. In El Salvador, the reactionary Alianza Republicana Nacionalista (ARENA) forces hold the reins of power but even with the support of the U.S., have been unable to defeat the revolutionaries. The FMLN showed its strength and popular support through its recent offensive in the capital city,[28] and its ability to assault the President's own neighbourhood.[29] So the "democrat" must negotiate with the progressive forces. But regionally, the "democrats" are increasingly right wing, and a trigger-happy U.S. is the wild card. The result, according to Carty, is "low intensity democracy."[30]

Paul Sweezy asserts that, "The 1990s will witness the disintegration of the worldwide U.S. empire and its probable replacement by a system of competing trade-and-currency blocs."[31] While this is likely, it could mean increasing pressure on Central America as the United States tries to reassert control over its historic "sphere of influence." After Panama, the Nicaraguans could not rule out a direct U.S. military intervention. And if the contras continued armed action and a "civil war" disrupted, the United States could intervene to save a fledgling "democracy," as the Sandinistas recognized. One FSLN leader, Victor Tirado, has gone so far as to argue that the "cycle of anti-imperialist revolutions is over," and progressive forces will have to come to an accommodation with imperialists and find new ways to achieve revolutionary goals.[32]

With the changes in the East, revolutionaries in the Third World can no longer depend on the Soviets to come to their support. Cuba is increasingly put on the defensive, as the United States is becoming increasingly belligerent.[33] But invasions of Cuba and Nicaragua would not be as easy as the 1983 invasion of Grenada. And the new regimes have made too many gains to be turned back completely. Even the short experience of "the revo" in Grenada has left its impact, and the people have found the U.S. alternative to be no alternative.[34]

The United States could not even invade Panama and overthrow its ruler without impunity. A visiting Brazilian priest, Fr. Ramaces Hartwig, alerted us to the fact that the United States waited for the results of the recent election in Brazil before undertaking the invasion of Panama. When the right-wing candidate, Fernando Collor, defeated the left-wing "Lula" (Luis Inacio da Silva), the United States went ahead with its invasion without fear of opposition from Brazil, the region's most powerful State. This reveals that the popular forces have gained real strength in Brazil and throughout Latin America, and within Panama itself the U.S. invaders met stiff opposition.[35] FDR leader Ruben Zamora remarked over two years ago that low intensity warfare was not working for the United States in El Salvador.[36]

So in Nicaragua the new right-wing government must dialogue with the left-wing opposition. In El Salvador both sides have admitted that a military end to the civil war is unlikely, and the FMLN has stated that its November 1989 offensive was intended to push negotiations.[37] And these negotiations have been pushed to the point that the ARENA government and the FMLN signed a September 25, 1991 accord which brings the warring parties in El Salvador, as one observer puts it, "to the brink of peace."[38] The upsurge of armed guerrilla activities in Guatemala is waged, according to the Unidad Revolucionaria Nacional de Guatemala (URNG), to make its "democratic" government more serious about negotiations and push the army, which holds the real power, to participate. The most immediate result has been, though, to push some sectors of the Guatemalan ruling class and army (some of the most reactionary groups on the planet) to call for a return to the "total war" of the early 1980s. But the popular sector has rebounded somewhat from that phase of terror, and some communities have even begun to refuse to participate in the so-called "civil defense patrols" which were initiated by the army as one measure to increase their control over the civilian population.[39]

The ruling class in Guatemala, along with its right-wing counterparts in El Salvador and Nicaragua, is divided over what means will achieve its ends. The balance of forces in the region might suggest a sort of interim social democratic compromise. But if this turns out to be a possibility, the problems of the region, and of the Third World in general, are too serious for it to be a long-term solution. The social structures of inequality generated by peripheral capitalism must be tackled head on. And the counterinsurgency States and death squads constructed to maintain those structures must be dismantled.[40]

Narco-Terrorism?

Again, the wild card is U.S. imperialism, and most recently the Bush administration has shown no great signs of favouring compromise. The November 1989 fighting in El Salvador ended Guatemala's "active neutrality" in regional foreign affairs, when "a U.S. Air Force Hercules 144 transport plane left Guatemala City for El Salvador, apparently carrying arms or soldiers. The French Press Agency (AFP) reported that 126 of Guatemala's elite counterinsurgency force 'Kaibiles' were transferred to El Salvador."[41] And in Guatemala itself White House moves appear to have been designed to damage the chances for the Christian Democratic presidential candidate, Alfonso Cabrera, in the fall, 1990 elections, in favour of one of the more reactionary candidates.[42] The winner was Jorge Serrano Elias, an evangelical businessman.

In the "post-Cold War era," U.S. foreign policy has had to take a new tack. Gasperini asserts that "drugs have replaced communism as the prime 'enemy'."[43] The "Bush doctrine" appears to be a "war on drugs."[44] Here the target is the "narco-terrorist," or the "narco-guerrilla." In general terms, the doctrine fits a shift in recent years from chasing "communist" bogeymen to chasing "terrorists,"[45] such as Saddam Hussein. Terrorism is a more convenient term because it can easily encapsulate all manner of anti-imperialist forces and arouses a more emotive response than the now rather stale cry of "communism." But this is a subterfuge, as Chomsky and Herman have demonstrated in their various writings.[46] The real terror network is that of the United States and its client States, from the Philippines to South Africa to Israel to Latin America. And the real targets are still primarily left and progressive forces.

In Guatemala:

As far as the war on drugs is concerned, everyone here knows the real narco-terrorists are not the guerrillas, as the U.S. Embassy would like us to believe. As a former top government administrator accused of cocaine trafficking, Minera Navas, recently testified, the actual cocaine kingpins in Guatemala were the military high command, intelligence services, police forces and the current administration. However, the myth of URNG poppy fields gives the U.S. military and its affiliated mercenaries a handy excuse to spray poisonous herbicides over the food crops and forest cover of the guerrillas and their campesino supporters.[47]

This "drug war" is clearly a cover for a U.S. counterinsurgency campaign, as is most evident in the massive increase of U.S. personnel and "aid" being sent to the Andean countries of South America where, especially in Colombia and Peru, there have been active guerrilla insurgencies for years.[48] The mainstream media give us almost daily reports on the situation in Colombia, the largest supplier of narcotics to the United States. The picture we are given is one of constant conflict between the "white knights" of law and order and the "black knights" of terrorist drug cartels. But behind the façade we discover: "Drug wars are intra-elite skirmishes; the real fight is with the guerrillas."[49]

There is a double class character to these skirmishes and fights. The State comes down heaviest on the lower middle-class Medellín cartel, for example, than on the more respectable upper middle-class Cali cartel, both of whom are jockeying for political power. These skirmishes go in cycles, and as each fades "the enhanced military and police powers [are] employed against the left, the guerrillas, and popular organizations."[50] And the "drug lords" are just as involved in the "dirty war" against the popular forces as is the State.

According to the Colombian defense minister:

> The most important issue facing the forces of public order is the confrontations with the cartels of Cali and Medellín. But there is a third cartel which is politically and socially more pernicious, harmful and dangerous for the institutional stability of the country. That cartel is the FARC [Frente Armado Revolucionario de Colombia].[51]

But for U.S. rulers, confusing the Left with the drug trade provides a convenient ruse for stepping up counterinsurgency campaigns in a way that can be more easily sold to the U.S. population, thus circumventing the "Vietnam Syndrome." And basking in the immediate afterglow of his "victory" in the Gulf War, George Bush boasted that the United States could "kick the Vietnam Syndrome once and for all." But what kind of victory is this?

Anti-imperialist Struggle and the Gulf War

The Iraqi invasion of Kuwait in August of 1990 became an excuse for the United States and its allies to invade Iraq in January of 1991, under the guise of United Nations' sponsorship. The ensuing events continue to have important implications for the Third World.

These movements face two clear difficulties. The former Soviet Union and China, faced by their own internal problems and attempts at some sort of reincorporation into the capitalist world economy, will no longer unequivocally stand up and defend Third World revolutions, even diplomatically. So once again it seems the United Nations has become a tool of the West. Western journalists are delighted that the United Nations is once again "effective." But even they are confused as to when they should say "U.N." or "U.S."

The second problem for Third World movements is a political-economic one. Third World economies are in such deplorable shape, with debt crises and increasing dependency structures being crafted at the behest of the International Monetary Fund and the World Bank, that most Third World regimes simply knuckled under to U.S. demands to support the "allies" in their Gulf War in return for promises of economic benefits. The lesson for other Third World States is that they will suffer a fate similar to Iraq's, economically if not militarily, if they step too far out of line.[52]

So these may look like bad times, but the longer view makes it obvious that capitalism has little of benefit to offer the Third World. Extreme misery and continuing debt crisis is the order of the day. Even our social life is coming to take on more of a Third World aura.[53]

The Chinese word for "Crisis" can also be translated as "opportunity." And Mao Zedong said that the crises of the First and Second World Wars produced the Soviet and Chinese revolutions. There are opportunities in the present crisis as well. The escalation of aggression against the Third World, combined with assaults on labour and the welfare State at home, could bring together First and Third World struggles. The emperor will be seen once more to have no clothes. And this will be the first step for many on the road to freedom. According to Bush the war is over but, more likely, it has only just begun. While Bush boasts of a new world order, the political fallout from this war promises to be incredible.

Socialism, or the End of History?

The U.S. is under pressure from various sides. A wave of pro-democracy sentiment is washing over the globe. We in the West are informed (more often *mis*informed) about struggles in the East. But there are democratic successes throughout the South as well. Along with Latin American examples already discussed, we should note those of Mexico, where popular opposition to the long-reigning Partido Revolucionario Institucional (PRI) State has grown, and opposition critics claim that the coalition headed by Cuauhtemoc Cardenas was cheated out of its 1988 electoral victory by a fraudulent vote count; Haiti, where slave revolts gave rise to the first independent State in Latin America in 1804, and where more recent popular opposition routed the Duvalier dictatorship, and eventually brought liberation theologist Jean-Bertrand Aristide to the presidency;[54] South Africa, where the popular forces and international pressures have pushed the rulers to begin negotiations with the African National Congress (ANC) over the dismantling of apartheid; Israel, where another apartheid State has been unable to repress the Palestinian "intifada"; the Philippines, where Corazon Aquino's "democracy" is subject to coup upon coup as the power elite squabble over their inability to squash the New People's Army (NPA) and other popular forces and the campaign against the presence of U.S military bases (see Chapter Six); and less prominent cases such as Uganda, where the National Resistance Movement (NRM) under the leadership of Yoweri Museveni has begun to bring "the jewel of Africa" out of a long night of dictatorships;[55] Zaire where the 26-year-old dictatorship of Mobutu Sese Seko is crumbling; and Nepal, where a pro-democracy movement, which includes communists, has forced the 30 year old autocratic monarchy into a democratic opening.[56] These struggles might not lead to the socialist conclusion we may have expected some years ago. But even an interim social democratic compromise is a step forward. And "the end of the Cold War" might bring some positive results, as in Ethiopia, where the downfall of an unpopular Soviet-backed regime gives some breathing space to popular liberation movements, such as the Eritrean People's Liberation Front (EPLF).

The problem is that we do not really know what socialism is. Even in eastern Europe, where the rhetoric is that of "anti-communism" and "anti-socialism," there are no clear ideas on which way to go. While there is movement toward the adoption of market policies and many Western ideas, many are cautious about their new relations with the West.[57] In eastern Germany, for example, people are wary about losing their social rights such as guaranteed child care for working mothers.[58]

In the West as well there are growing popular movements for social justice. Some real innovations in more communal forms have been affected, especially by the most exploited and oppressed sectors of our societies.[59] And these experiments will likely increase as the powerful continue to push their neoconservative/neoliberal policies that lead to a sort of peripheralization of the center, with increasing social inequality, unemployment, homelessness, et cetera.[60] It is clear that, for growing numbers of people in both center and periphery, capitalism has *not* delivered the goods.[61] And, despite all the self-serving rhetoric about a "triumph of capitalism," arguments as to why socialism is necessary are still valid.[62]

As the U.S. continues to decline and the capitalist world breaks up into rival economic blocs, Petras notes a shift on the part of some of the U.S power elite "from geopolitical confrontations in the East and South for ideological hegemony, to economic rivalries within the West for global market shares."[63] Their policies give a high profile to State subsidies for exports, while continuing to preach deficit reduction. This will mean "cutting social programs to 'remain internationally competitive'," thus further exacerbating the problems of the working class.

Growing economic problems combined with already growing demands for disarmament and environmental programs, spell a much different social order than that of capitalism. But constructing this social order will take a long time. It will require a process of *"disalienation"*[64] to create Che Guevara's socialist "new man" (sic) in order to "undo" the mentality that developed with capitalism. In the latter case, Magdoff and

Sweezy discuss how the shaping of a "human nature" fit to operate such a system, the possessive individuals of classical political economy, "did not just appear one fine day to run the new economy. It took generations to create them."[65]

We live in confused and confusing times, where black and white often seem to blend into grey. With Galeano

> I sometimes feel as though they have stolen even our words. The term 'socialism' is applied in the West as make-up for injustice; in Eastern Europe, it evokes purgatory or maybe hell.... In our time, the bureaucrats have stigmatized hope and besmirched the most beautiful of human adventures; but I also believe that socialism is not Stalinism.... And today more than ever it is necessary to dream. To dream, together, dreams that undream themselves and become incarnate in mortal matter.... This is my testimony. A dinosaur's confession? Perhaps. In any case, it is the affirmation of one who believes that the human condition is not doomed to selfishness and the obscene pursuit of money, and that socialism did not die, because it had not yet been — that today is the first day of the long life before it.[66]

While many on the Left are jumping ship and drifting into "post-marxism," or some other form of liberalism,[67] socialism is still the best term to describe the uncharted waters leading to a better world. Perhaps now that some of the counterfeit and bogus versions of socialism are out of the way, we can get on with struggles for the real thing. For, as global capitalism continues to produce the conditions for militarism, environmental destruction, and destitution of the people of the world, more than ever the choice appears to be between "socialism" and "barbarism."

Notes

1. Francis Fukuyama, "The End of History?," *The National Interest*, Vol 16, Summer 1989: 3-17.
2. Carl Marzani, "On Interring Communism and Exalting Capitalism," *Monthly Review*, Vol. 41, No. 8, January 1990: pp. 1-32.
3. V.I. Lenin, *Collected Works*, Vol. 38. Moscow: Progress Publishers, 1915.

4. Marx and Engels, among others, have discussed the contradictory character of, for example, the peasantry. See Terry R. Kandal, "Marx and Engels on International Relations, Revolution, and Counterrevolution," in M.T. Martin & T.R. Kandal (eds.), *Studies of Development and Change In The Modern World*. New York: Oxford University Press, 1989, pp. 25-76. For more recent discussions of anti-systemic struggles see Samir Amin, Giovanni Arrighi, Andre Gunder Frank and Immanuel Wallerstein, *Transforming the Revolution: Social Movements and the World-System*. New York: Monthly Review Press, 1990; and Giovanni Arrighi, Terence K. Hopkins, and Immanuel Wallerstein, *Antisystemic Movements*. London: Verso Books, 1989.
5. For a good discussion see Hans Koning, *Columbus: His Enterprise*. New York: Monthly Review Press, 1991. We might distinguish here between the "old" imperialism of mercantilism, and the "new" imperialism of "monopoly capital." See Harry Magdoff, *Imperialism: From the Colonial Age to the Present*. New York: Monthly Review Press, 1978. On the other hand, even some on the left argue against the importance of imperialism, eg., Alain Lipietz, *Mirages and Miracles: The Crises of Global Fordism*. London: Verso Books, 1987. For a critique of that argument see Dave Broad, "Fordism and Imperialism", *Monthly Review*, Vol. 41, No. 10, March 1990: pp. 52-8; and Prabhat Patnaik, "Whatever Happened to Imperialism?," *Monthly Review*, Vol. 42, No. 6, November 1990: pp. 1-6.
6. Paul Sweezy, "Questions on the Transition to Socialism," *Studies in Political Economy* No. 18, Fall 1985: pp. 9-12.
7. Robert Heilbroner, 1989 "Reflections: The Triumph of Capitalism," *The New Yorker* Vol. 64, January 23, 1989: pp. 98-109.
8. Paul Sweezy, "Nineteen Eighty-Nine," *Monthly Review*, Vol. 41, No. 1, April 1990: pp. 18-21. Some might suggest that 1991 be added to Sweezy's list, but others would argue that the events of 1991 are part of a "post-Cold War era" that began in 1989. See Noam Chomsky and David Barsamian, "Noam Chomsky on the 'New World Order' and the Origins of His Scepticism," *Our Generation*, Vol. 22, No. 1/2, Spring 1991. pp. 16-74.
9. Daniel Singer, "On Revolution," *Monthly Review*, Vol. 41, No. 2, June 1989: pp. 33-6.
10. William Gasperini, "Did End Justify Means in Panama Invasion?," *In These Times*, January 17-23, 1990: pp. 11, 22.
11. Michael T. Klare and Peter Kornbluh (eds.), *Low Intensity Warfare: Counterinsurgency, Proinsurgency, and Antiterrorism in the Eighties*. New York: Pantheon Books, 1988.
12. CIC (Center for International Communications), *Reagan's Freedom Fighters: The Remaking of Somocista Terror*. Managua: Center for International Communications, 1984. CIC, *Covert War Terror*. Managua: Center for International Communications, 1985. Dieter Eich and Carlos Rincon, *The Contras: Interviews with Anti-Sandinistas*. San Francisco: Synthesis Publications, 1985.
13. Nancy Murray, "Mozambique: The Revolution and the Bandits, an Interview with Lina Magaia," *Race & Class*, Vol. 30, No. 4, April-June 1989: pp. 21-9.
14. Carol B. Thompson, "War By Another Name: Destabilization in Nicaragua and Mozambique," *Race & Class*, Vol. 29, No. 4, Spring 1988: pp. 21-44.
15. *Canadian Dimension*, Vol. 24, No. 3, April/May 1990, p. 8
16. Africa News, "Angola Electioneering Starts in U.S.," *The Guardian*, Vol. 44, No. 2, October 30, 1991: p. 12.
17. For background to the southern African cases see John Saul, "The Southern African Revolution," in R. Miliband, L. Panitch and J. Saville (eds.), *The Socialist Register, 1989*. London: Merlin Press, 1989, pp. 47-73; and the special issue of *Southern Africa Report*, Vol. 4, October, 1988, on "States of Siege."

18. Susanne Jonas and Nancy Stein (eds.), *Democracy in Latin America: Visions and Realities*. New York: Bergin and Garvey Publishers, 1990.
19. Edward S. Herman and Frank Brodhead, *Demonstration Elections*. Boston: South End Press, 1984.
20. Dave Broad, "Central America: Elections versus Democracy," *Briarpatch*, Vol. 13, No. 5, June 1984: pp. 28-30.
21. See Chapter One.Slovo notes that the opponents of socialism "conveniently ignore the fact that most of the countries which tried to create conditions for the building of socialism faced unending civil war, aggression and externally-inspired banditry; a situation in which it is hardly possible to build any kind of stable social formation — capitalist or socialist." Joe Slovo, *Has Socialism Failed?* London: Inkululeko Publications, 1990.
22. John Newsinger, "Revolution and Counterrevolution: The Case of Finland in 1917-18," *Monthly Review*, Vol. 41, No. 10, March 1990: pp. 23-32.
23. *The Globe and Mail*, "Military Victory Called Impossible", Saturday, November 18, 1989.
24. Dennis Forkin, "From Montezuma to the Shores of Tripoli," *Canadian Dimension* Vol. 24, No. 2, March 1990: p. 33.
25. Arthur D. Kahn, "Was There No Superstructure in Ancient Rome?", *Monthly Review*, Vol. 41, No. 9, February 1990: p.38.
26. Karen Gellen, "A Salvadoran Rebel on Socialism's Upheaval," *The Guardian* Vol. 42, No. 19, March 7, 1990: pp. 15, 19. Joaquin Villalobos, "A Democratic Revolution for El Salvador," *Foreign Policy* No. 74, Spring 1989: pp. 103-22.
27. Even before taking office, president-elect Violeta Barrios de Chamorro's UNO forces began squabbling over policies and positions. UNO is a motley crew running from extreme right contras to the Communist Party, and united only by their opposition to the Sandinistas. With allies who see Chamorro as "a person of few intellectual resources who is incapable of governing the country in a crisis", and say: "It's possible that Violeta is not too bright" (*Globe and Mail*, 22/02/90), she has had a rough ride. If U.S. rulers think they have found Nicaragua's Corazon Aquino, they should know that Aquino is now under siege from both the left and her own right-wing supporters, who are given U.S. backing to keep Aquino in line.
28. Sara Miles and Bob Ostertag, "El Salvador: The Offensive in Perspective," *NACLA Report on the Americas*, Vol. 23, No. 6, April 1990: pp. 7-9.
29. Globe and Mail, "Rebels Raid Near Home of Salvadoran Leader," *The Globe and Mail*, Thursday, May 3, 1990.
30. Bob Carty, "LID: Low Intensity Democracy," *This Magazine*, Vol. 24, September, 1990: pp. 19-21.
31. Paul Sweezy, "U.S. Imperialism in the 1990s," *Monthly Review* Vol. 41, No. 5, October 1989: pp. 1-17.
32. Barricada, "Cycle of Anti-imperialist Revolutions is Over," *The Guardian* Vol. 42, No. 27, May 2, 1990: p. 13.
33. Globe and Mail, "Cuba Mobilizing in Wake of U.S. Military Exercises, *The Globe and Mail*, Friday, May 4, 1990.
34. Kathy McAfee, "Grenada: The Revo in Reverse," *NACLA Report on the Americas* Vol. 23, No. 5, February, 1990: pp. 27-32.
35. On the ferocity of the U.S. invasion of Panama, and resistance to it, see Brian Becker and Esmeralda Brown, "U.S. Wields Old-Style Colonial Power in Panama," *The Guardian*, Vol. 42, No. 20, March 14, 1990; Raul Leis, "Panama: The Other Side of Midnight," *NACLA Report On The Americas*, Vol. 23, No. 6, April, 1990: pp. 4-6; and

James Petras, "Eight Myths About Panama," *In These Times*, January 17-23, 1990: pp. 12-3, 22.

36. Jack Colhoun, "Ruben Zamora: 'Low Intensity Warfare Hasn't worked for U.S.'," *The Guardian* Vol. 40, No. 19, March 8, 1989: p. 13.
37. Mike Zielinski, "A Break through for Peace in El Salvador?", *The Guardian*, Vol. 42, No. 25, April 18, 1990: p. 12.
38. Marcella Tardy, "El Salvador on the Brink of Peace", *The Guardian*, Vol. 43, No. 44, October 9, 1991: pp. 10-11.
39. On the current situation in Guatemala see John Reed, "Guatemala's Reign of Misery", *The Guardian*, Vol. 42, No. 25, April 18, 1990: pp. 10-11; Philip Vine, "Guatemalan Army Changes Tack and Targets Popular Organizations", *Peace Courier* No. 3: pp. 8-9, 1990; and *Guatemala Update*, Toronto, Spring 1990.
40. Ruy Mauro Marini, "The Question of The State in the Latin American Class Struggle," *Contemporary Marxism*, No. 1, Spring, 1980: pp. 1-9.
41. *Guatemala Update*, Spring 1990.
42. John Reed, "Guatemala's Reign of Misery," *The Guardian*, Vol. 42, No. 25, April 18, 1990: pp. 10-1.
43. William Gasperini, "Did End Justify Means in Panama Invasion?," *In These Times*, January 17-23, 1990: pp. 11, 22.
44. However, "anti-communism" has had, and will continue to have its place in the imperialist repertoire. See Ralph Miliband, John Saville, and Marcel Liebman (eds.), *The Socialist Register*, 1984. London: Merlin Press, 1984.
45. Remember that as vice president Bush ran a "Task Force on Combating Terrorism", which oversaw the operations of Oliver North's "Office to Combat Terrorism." Peter Dale Scott, "Northwards without North: Bush, Counterterrorism, and the Continuation of Secret Power," *Social Justice*, Vol. 16, No. 2, Summer 1989: pp. 1-30.
46. See Noam Chomsky and Edward S. Herman, *The Political Economy of Human Rights* (2 Vols.). Montréal, Black Rose Books, 1979; Edward S. Herman, *The Real Terror Network: Terrorism in Fact and Propaganda*. Montréal: Black Rose Books, 1982; Noam Chomsky, *The Culture of Terrorism*. Montréal: Black Rose Books, 1988; and the special double issue (27/28) of *Social Justice* (1987) on "Contragate and Counterterrorism: A Global Perspective."
47. John Reed, "Guatemala's Reign of Misery", *The Guardian*, Vol. 42, No. 25, April 18, 1990: pp. 10-1.
48. But the war against "narco-guerrillas" has become the rage throughout the Americas. For example, a recent issue of the Belize government magazine *Belize Today* (August 1991) includes an article entitled "BDF [Belize Defence Force] Prepared to Fight Narco-guerrillas." Once a British colony, since its independence in 1981 the Central American country of Belize has rapidly been pulled into the U.S. orbit and is currently trying to curry favor with the United States by participating in Bush's drug wars. Dave Broad, "Belize — On the Rim of the Cauldron", *Monthly Review*, Vol. 35, No. 9, February 1984: pp.38-47.
49. Marc W. Chernick, "The Drug War," *NACLA Report on the Americas*, Vol. 23, No. 6, April, 1990: p. 30. For more on Colombia and other Latin American cases, see James Cockcroft, *Neighbors in Turmoil: Latin America*. New York: Harper and Row, 1989.
50. Marc W. Chernick, "The Drug War," *NACLA Report on the Americas*, Vol. 23, No. 6, April 1990: p. 31.
51. Cited in Marc W. Chernick, "The Drug War," *NACLA Report on the Americas*, Vol. 23, No. 6, April 1990: pp. 37-38.
52. Noam Chomsky, "U.S. Warns Third World: 'Don't Raise Your Heads'," *The Guardian* Vol. 42, No. 23, April 3, 1991: p. 18.

53. Dave Broad, "Peripheralization of the Centre: W(h)ither Canada?," *Alternate Routes*, No. 8, Fall 1988: pp. 1-41. Arthur MacEwan, "Why the Emperor Can't Afford New Clothes: International Change and Fiscal Disorder in the United States," *Monthly Review*, Vol. 43, No. 3, July—August 1991: pp. 74-94.
54. At the time of writing, Aristide has been deposed by a military junta, but popular opposition to the junta is so strong that the Organization of American States (OAS) has imposed sanctions, and even U.S. President Bush, whose chosen candidate for the Haitian presidency, Marc Bazin, was defeated by the Aristide forces, has declared that Aristide must be returned to office, though Bush's actions have not matched his words.
55. Rosalind Boyd, "The Struggle for Democracy: Uganda's National Resistance Movement", *Canadian Dimension*, Vol. 23, No. 6, September 1989: pp. 29-35.
56. Sunita, "Protesters Seize Power from Nepal's King," *The Guardian*, Vol. 42, No. 27, May 2, 1990: p. 16.
57. A common fallacy, found on the right and left, is the equation of market principles with capitalism. Anthropologists remind us that there are different types of markets which existed long before capitalism (see, eg., Richard Hodges, *Primitive and Peasant Markets*. Oxford: Basil Blackwell, 1988). So we should not assume that post-capitalist societies will not have market aspects, or that adoption of market policies implies a return to capitalism per se. An alternate view is that socialism will entail a combination of planning *and* market policies. (Howard Sherman, "The Second Soviet Revolution", *Monthly Review*, Vol. 41, No. 10, March 1990: pp. 14-22.)
58. Bruce Allen, "Unions in the GDR", *Our Times*, Vol. 9, No. 2, April 1990: pp. 18-21.
59. A. Sivanandan, "All That Melts Into Air Is Solid: The Hokum of New Times", *Race & Class*, Vol. 31, No. 3, January-March 1990: pp. 1-30.
60. Dave Broad, "Peripheralization of the Centre: W(h)ither Canada?," *Alternate Routes* No. 8, Fall 1988: pp. 1-41.
61. Vincente Navarro, "Historical Triumph: Capitalism or Socialism?," *Monthly Review*, Vol. 41, No. 6, November 1989: pp. 37-50.
62. Leo Huberman, "Why Socialism is Necessary," *Monthly Review*, Vol. 20, No. 8, January 1969: pp. 1-14.
63. There must, though, be conflict among U.S. rulers over this shift for, as we have seen, the Bush administration has not abandoned the right-wing policy of rolling back revolutions. See Thomas Bodenheimer and Robert Gould, *Rollback!: Right-wing Power in U.S. Foreign Policy*. Boston: South End Press, 1989; and Chapter Two above. James Petras, "U.S. Takes Aim at Capitalist Rivals," *The Guardian* Vol. 42, No. 25, April 18, 1990: p. 17.
64. Samir Amin, *Class and Nation, Historically and in the Current Crisis*. New York: Monthly Review Press, 1980.
65. Paul Sweezy, "Nineteen Eighty-Nine," *Monthly Review*, Vol. 41, No. 11, April, 1990: pp. 18-21.
66. Eduardo Galeano, "A Child Lost in the Storm," *The Guardian*, Vol. 42, No. 27, May, 1990: pp. 1, 12.
67. A. Sivanandan, "All That Melts Into Air Is Solid: The Hokum of New Times," *Race & Class*, Vol. 31, No. 3, January-March 1990: pp. 1-30.

New From BLACK ROSE BOOKS

IMAGINING THE MIDDLE EAST
by Thierry Hentsch
Translated by Fred A. Reed

Thierry Hentsch examines how the Western perception of the Middle East was formed and how we have used these perceptions as a rationalization for setting policies and determining actions. The book concludes with the consequence of this imagination on the Gulf war and its aftermath.

256 pages
Paper ISBN: 1-895431-12-3 $19.95 / Cloth ISBN: 1-895431-13-1 $38.95

BOOKS BY NOAM CHOMSKY

ON POWER AND IDEOLOGY

These five lectures on U.S. international and security policy examine the persistent features of U.S. foreign policy; the overall framework of order; Central America and its place in the foreign policy pattern; U.S. national security policy and how it affects foreign and domestic policies; and the domestic scene in the U.S.

146 pages
Paper ISBN: 0-921689-04-7 $14.95 / Cloth ISBN: 0-921689-05-5 $34.95

TURNING THE TIDE
The U.S. and Latin America
2nd revised edition

Chomsky analyses the aims and effect of U.S. policy in Central America, examining both the historical record and more recent events.

The degree to which Mr. Chomsky cannot only challenge, but also persuasively reverse claims about those forces responsible for the worst repression and aggression in Central America should jolt any fair-minded person who still buys the Administration's moral case for current U.S. policy.
New York Times

300 pages
Paper ISBN: 0-920057-91-8 $16.95 / Cloth ISBN: 0-920057-90-X $38.95

PIRATES & EMPERORS
International Terrorism in the Real World

This work deals with terrorism, both State and 'retail', with special attention given to the scandal surrounding the Iranian arms deal. Chomsky criticises U.S. foreign policy and the American media, focusing on the Middle East.

...raises provocative questions about U.S. diplomacy.
Maclean's

206 pages
Paper ISBN: 0-920057-93-4 $14.95 / Cloth ISBN: 0-920557-92-6 $36.95

RADICAL PRIORITIES
edited by Carlos P. Otero
2nd revised edition, 4th printing

For those who desire a fuller picture of Chomsky's fascinating political scholarship, his Radical Priorities *is to be recommended.*
Harvard International Review

307 pages
Paper ISBN: 0-920057-17-9 $18.95 / Cloth ISBN: 0-920057-16-0 $38.95

has also published the following books of related interests:

The Anarchist Papers, *Dimitrios Roussopoulos, ed.*
The Radical Papers, *Dimitrios Roussopoulos, ed.*
The Culture of Terrorism, *Noam Chomsky*
Language and Politics, *Noam Chomsky*
The Political Economy of Human Rights, Vol. 1: *The Washington Connection and Third World Fascism, Noam Chomsky and Edward S. Herman*
The Political Economy of Human Rights, Vol. 2: *After the Cataclysm: Postwar Indochina and the Reconstruction of Imperial Ideology, Noam Chomsky and Edward S. Herman*
The Real Terror Network: *Terrorism in Fact and Propaganda, Edward S. Herman*
The Iran-Contra Connection, *Jonathon Marshall, Peter Dale Scott, and Jane Hunter*
The Politics of Euro-Communism, *Carl Boggs and David Plotke, eds.*
The Modern State: *An Anarchist Analysis, Frank Harrison*
Post-Scarcity Anarchism, *Murray Bookchin*
Bakunin on Anarchism, *Sam Dolgoff, ed.*
The Cuban Revolution: *A Critical Perspective, Sam Dolgoff*
Voices From Tiananmen Square: *Beijing Spring and the Democracy Movement, Mok Chiu Yu and J. Frank Harrison, eds.*
Nationalism and the National Question, *Nicole Arnaud and Jacques Dofny*
World Inequality, *Immanuel Wallerstein, ed.*
The State, *Franz Oppenheimer*
Anarchist Organization: *The History of the F.A.I., Juan Gòmez Casas*
Toward an Ecological Society, *Murray Bookchin*
Indignant Heart: *A Black Worker's Journal, Charles Denby*
The Great French Revolution, *Peter Kropotkin*
Mexico: *Land and Liberty, Ricardo Flores Magon*
The Bolsheviks and Workers' Control 1917-1921, *Maurice Brinton*

Send for our free complete catalogue of books
BLACK ROSE BOOKS
C.P. 1258
Succ. Place du Parc
Montréal, Québec H2W 2R3
(514) 844-4076

Printed by the workers of
Ateliers Graphiques Marc Veilleux Inc.
for
Black Rose Books Ltd.